VANCOUVER EXPOSED

VANCOUVER EXPOSED

SEARCHING FOR THE CITY'S **HIDDEN HISTORY**

EVE LAZARUS

ARSENAL PULP PRESS
VANCOUVER

VANCOUVER EXPOSED

ARSENAL PULP PRESS
Suite 202 – 211 East Georgia St.
Vancouver, BC V6A 1Z6
Canada
arsenalpulp.com

The publisher gratefully acknowledges the support of the Canada Council for the Arts and the British Columbia Arts Council for its publishing program, and the Government of Canada, and the Government of British Columbia (through the Book Publishing Tax Credit Program), for its publishing activities.

The author gratefully acknowledges the financial support of the Yosef Wosk Publication Fund at Vancouver Heritage Foundation.

Arsenal Pulp Press acknowledges the xʷməθkʷəy̓əm (Musqueam), Sḵwx̱wú7mesh (Squamish) and səl̓ilwətaʔɬ (Tsleil-Waututh) Nations, custodians of the traditional, ancestral and unceded territories where our office is located. We pay respect to their histories, traditions and continuous living cultures and commit to accountability, respectful relations and friendship.

COVER IMAGE BY Canadian Photo Co., City of Vancouver Archives, Bu P726
COVER AND INTERIOR DESIGN BY Jazmin Welch
BACK COVER PHOTOGRAPHS TOP TO BOTTOM BY Tom Carter collection, John Denniston photo, NVMA 15806, courtesy Lisa Pantages
PHOTOGRAPHS FOR CHAPTER OPENERS BY Catherine Rose
EDITED BY Shirarose Wilensky
COPY EDITED BY Derek Fairbridge
PROOFREAD BY Alison Strobel
INDEXED BY Stephen Ullstrom

Printed and bound in Canada

LIBRARY AND ARCHIVES CANADA CATALOGUING IN PUBLICATION:
Title: Vancouver exposed : searching for the city's hidden history / Eve Lazarus.
Names: Lazarus, Eve, author.
Identifiers: Canadiana (print) 20200211501 | Canadiana (ebook) 20200211552 |
   ISBN 9781551528298 (softcover) | ISBN 9781551528304 (HTML)
Subjects: LCSH: Vancouver (B.C.)—History. | LCSH: Vancouver (B.C.)—Buildings, structures, etc.—
   History. | LCSH: Neighborhoods—British Columbia—Vancouver—History. | LCSH: Vancouver
   (B.C.)—History—Pictorial works. | LCSH: Vancouver (B.C.)—Buildings, structures, etc.—History—
   Pictorial works. | LCSH: Neighborhoods—British Columbia Vancouver—History—Pictorial works.
Classification: LCC FC3847.4 .L39 2020 | DDC 971.1/33—dc23

CONTENTS

INTRODUCTION

I started my blog *Every Place Has a Story* in 2010 as a way to add to stories from my first book, *At Home with History: The Untold Secrets of Greater Vancouver's Heritage Homes*. The blog quickly became my obsession, and I looked forward to digging into a new story every week. When people asked me what my blog was about, I told them it was about history and heritage houses and murder. But that really meant anything I thought was interesting—from street photographers to ghosts, research tips to legendary women, and others who are typically not found on the front page of newspapers.

Later I started the *Every Place Has a Story* Facebook page and soon I was connecting with bloggers, tour guides, artists, academics and amateur historians who shared a love for Vancouver's quirks and the city's often seedy history. Gradually people started to post comments and personal anecdotes from their own family histories, and little by little the stories took on new life. These observations and memories, as well as photos scanned from family albums, then helped shape the direction of this book.

Early in 2019, I mentioned to Arsenal Pulp publisher Brian Lam that my blog was approaching its tenth anniversary, and I was thinking of self-publishing a book of my stories. Brian said Arsenal might be interested and asked me to send him a proposal. I did, and I am thrilled that this is the result.

Vancouver Exposed is not meant to be read from start to finish. It jumps from walled-up sculptures to missing murals to repurposed buildings. There are crashes, explosions, scary institutions and crimes. There are amazing athletes, squatters, architects and a sea captain. There are stories of big plans that never happened, missing theatres, a fake house and not-so-secret tunnels.

The book is divided into six areas, starting with what's always been one of the city's most important intersections, Granville and West Georgia.

There are still regal old buildings dotting the area around that intersection, and over the years, I've been in and out of several of them—the Hudson's Bay department store, the Vancouver Art Gallery, the Hotel Vancouver and the Hotel Georgia. I may have even noticed the three nurses looking down from their eleventh-storey parapets on the Georgia Medical-Dental Building, but it wasn't until the early part of this century that I gave any thought to these buildings, or what was there before them. Much later, when I fell in love with Vancouver's sleazy underbelly and dwindling heritage, I found that our civic enthusiasm for pulling things down has always been with us. In fact, it's astounding when you think in terms of not what we've lost but what we've struggled to retain.

The section about the Downtown Eastside includes stories that explore how Hastings Street evolved from the "Great White Way" to our current mess. It looks at Woodward's department store's forgotten elevator operators, Christmas window displays and $1.49 Day, and travels through tunnels, stations and terminals.

In the West End section we have the much-loved English Bay lifeguard and swimming teacher Joe Fortes, successful salon and beauty school owner Maxine MacGilvray, the English Bay Pier, the Hippocampus fish and chip shop and the distinctive Stuart Building. The neighbourhood is still home to the century-old Polar Bear Swim, a long-forgotten cemetery and several of Vancouver's buried houses.

In the section of the book that encompasses the city west of Main Street, there are ghost signs on buildings to remind us of businesses past, and there are the houses of Downtown South, that mostly exist only in memory. There is an exotic museum that is now a record store, a former bootlegging joint turned restaurant and a sheet-metal rocket ship.

In the section about what lies east of Main Street there's Chuck Currie's red-and-white polka-dotted house, an infant memorial garden, an axe murder, the annual summer spectacle of the Pacific National Exhibition and the Japanese internment camps at Hastings Park.

The North Vancouver section features a murder in a convent and a monument to remember the atrocities of the residential school system. Just across Burrard Inlet from downtown Vancouver, Canada's oldest nudist camp, an annual belly flop competition and an inn that has served as a resort, a brothel and an illegal gambling establishment are all fair game.

Got your own story about Vancouver's hidden history, or something to add? Post a comment on my blog, or get in touch at *info@evelazarus.com*. I'd love to hear from you!

DOWNTOWN

WE HELD A FUNERAL FOR THE BIRKS BUILDING

The protestors are wearing *Video Armour* crocheted out of used videotapes collected from television and film studios by artist Evelyn Roth.

Angus McIntyre photo, 1974

At two p.m. on Sunday, March 24, 1974, a group of about 100 people, many of them students and professors from the University of British Columbia School of Architecture, came together in a mock funeral for the Birks Building, an eleven-storey Edwardian masterpiece at Georgia and Granville with a terracotta facade and a curved front corner.

Participants marched from the old Vancouver Art Gallery at Georgia and Thurlow, led by a police escort and accompanied by a New Orleans funeral band playing a sombre dirge. The mourners assembled under the Birks clock, an ornate iron timepiece that stood more than twenty feet (6.5 metres) tall and for decades had been a local landmark and familiar meeting place. For generations of Vancouverites, "Meet you at the Birks clock" was a common phrase.

On this day, it was too late to stop the demolition—it had already begun—but not too late to protest what author and historian Michael Kluckner and others have called an egregious act of architectural vandalism. The crew working on the new building across the road shut off the air compressors and laid down their tools. Reverend Jack Kent, chaplain of the Vancouver Mariners Club, officiated. A choir accompanied him.

Angus McIntyre, then twenty-six, grabbed his Konica Autoreflex T2 35mm camera and rode his bike downtown to record the event. "There was a gathering, a sharing of ideas, a choir performance and a laying of the wreaths," Angus told me. "A small group of people wearing recycled video-tape clothing put hexes on new buildings nearby. As soon as it came time to return to the art gallery, the band switched to Dixieland jazz, and the mood became slightly more upbeat."

And just like that, the beautiful old Birks Building—well not that old, really: it was only sixty-one in 1974—was killed off to make way for the Scotia Tower and Vancouver Centre Mall. For a long time afterward, a large RIP banner hung in the window of a second-storey office in the Sam Kee Building on Pender Street.

The only positive thing to come out of the loss of this much-loved building was that it mobilized Vancouver's heritage preservation community, who pressured city council to request heritage protection powers from the provincial government. This move saved many of the city's other fine historic structures—including the Orpheum Theatre, Hudson's Bay, Waterfront Station, the Hotel Vancouver and the Marine Building—from a similar fate.

In the 1970s, the Scotia Tower and Vancouver Centre development took out the Strand Theatre and the iconic Birks Building, an eleven-storey Edwardian edifice where generations of Vancouverites met under the clock.

Vancouver Archives Str N201.1, 1924

PACIFIC
CENTRE

When I moved to Vancouver from Australia in the mid-1980s, locals had already had a dozen years to get used to Pacific Centre and the "Great White Urinal"—the name they'd not so affectionately bestowed upon the Eaton's department store building. But it wasn't until several years ago when I saw a 1924 photo showing the Strand Theatre, the Birks Building and the second Hotel Vancouver lined up along Georgia at Granville, that I realized how much we had lost.

In the 1960s, the pro-development city council sought to launch a significant redevelopment of downtown Vancouver, with the intersection of Georgia and Granville Streets as the epicentre of this change. Many feared that the downtown core would lose business to the malls that were opening in the suburbs, and the hope was that a new, modern shopping centre would attract people to breathe life back into that intersection. This retail vibrancy would come, they believed, through a new and improved superblock and underground parking that spread across several blocks. The superblock was made up of Block 52—bounded by Granville, Georgia, Howe and Robson—and Block 42—bounded by Granville, Georgia, Howe and Dunsmuir. The problem was that the T. Eaton Company, which owned all of Block 52, didn't seem in a hurry to move their department store from its location on West Hastings Street (currently the SFU Harbour Centre building), and a new Eaton's was essential to anchor the proposed shopping mall. The other problem was that Block 42 was owned by eighteen individual landowners, and none of them wanted to sell. By the fifth redevelopment report in July 1964, a frustrated Mayor William Rathie and members of city council were trying to figure out ways

Angus McIntyre got this shot in 1974 by leaning out of an open arched window on the top floor of the Birks Building. The Granville Mall was under construction, and Eaton's had just opened.

Angus McIntyre photo

they could expropriate the land from the unwilling owners.

In May 1968, the city held a plebiscite to allow them to buy up all the properties in Block 42, and seventy percent of voters agreed. The subsequent mayor, Tom Campbell, told the press: "We've got a united city which wants a heart. Vancouver had only a past—today it has a future. This is Vancouver's greatest day."[1]

By 1974, the city had the Pacific Centre and Vancouver Centre shopping malls, much of it as an underground bunker. We'd rid the streets of grand old brick buildings and gained the IBM Tower, the former Four Seasons Hotel, the Scotia Tower and a thirty-storey black glass monument to capitalism in the TD Tower. Rather than revitalize the Granville and Georgia intersection, we had sucked the life right out of it.

ABOVE The newly bulldozed Block 42 in 1973 and the thirty-storey TD Tower replaced the parking lot that had replaced the second Hotel Vancouver in 1949, and Eaton's built a five-storey store. In 1981, Eaton's added another two floors. Later, the store became a Sears and, since 2015, has been a Nordstrom, a high-end American department store.
Vancouver Archives 23-24

RIGHT An aerial view showing the future site of Eaton Centre, Pacific Centre and Robson Square, ca. 1963.
Vancouver Archives 515-32

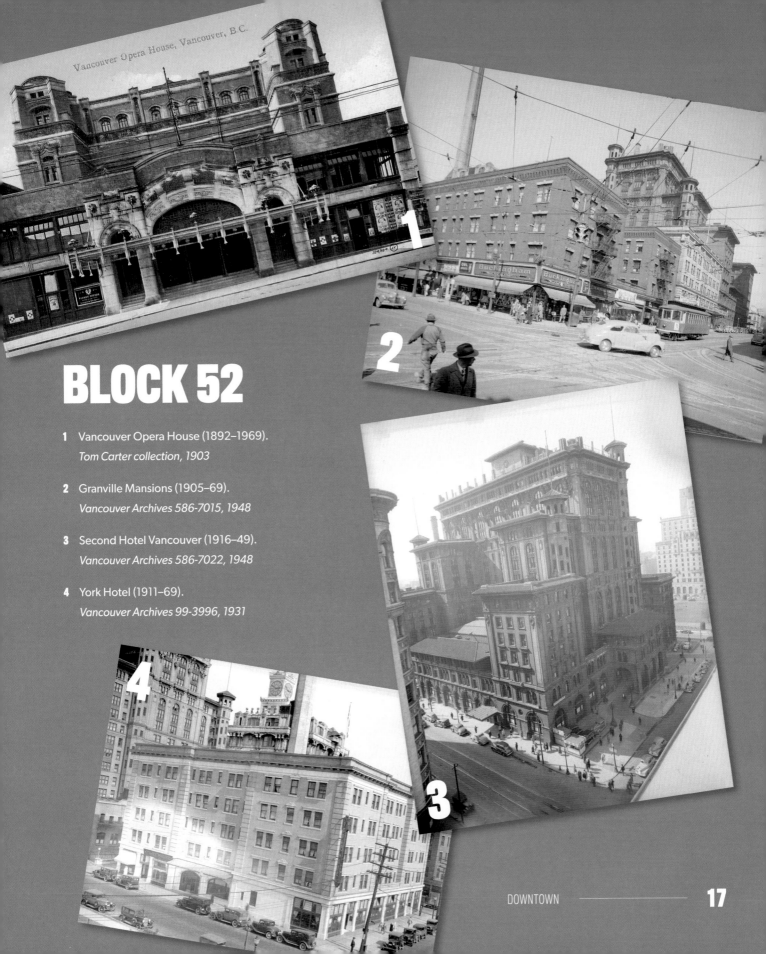

BLOCK 52

1 Vancouver Opera House (1892–1969).
Tom Carter collection, 1903

2 Granville Mansions (1905–69).
Vancouver Archives 586-7015, 1948

3 Second Hotel Vancouver (1916–49).
Vancouver Archives 586-7022, 1948

4 York Hotel (1911–69).
Vancouver Archives 99-3996, 1931

BLOCK 42

After the City of Vancouver declined to buy the park on the northwest corner of Georgia and Granville for $17,000, the Canadian Pacific Railway sold the lot to developers Benjamin Johnston and Samuel Howe who built the three-storey Johnston-Howe Block in 1901 and promptly flipped it for $1 million the following year.

1 The CPR Park and Bandstand at the corner of Georgia and Granville Streets, ca. 1900.
Vancouver Archives Str P33

2 Colonial Theatre (1899–1969).
Vancouver Archives 1135-46, 1957

3 Johnston-Howe Block (1900–69).
Vancouver Archives 99-4306, 1933

Howe Street—shown left of frame in this photo of downtown taken from the first Hotel Vancouver at Granville and Georgia, July 1, 1889—was once used for horse racing.
Vancouver Archives Van Sc P102.1

VANCOUVER'S FIRST HORSE RACE

The city's first official Dominion Day horse race was supposed to be held in 1887 along Granville Street. Unfortunately, it had rained too hard and conditions were too muddy, so the race moved to Howe Street. The starting line was just above Pacific Street and the finish line was at the first Hotel Vancouver (where the TD Tower is today). The Dominion Day race continued the following year with four horses contending—George Black's Bryan O'Lynn, Sam Brighouse's Coquitlam Jim, Charles Casell's Royal, and the Duke of York's Slow Dick. In 1892, the races officially moved to Hastings Park, where they remain.

THE FIRST CPR STATION

The first transcontinental train arrived in Vancouver in May 1887, and it was a very big deal. Businesses closed for the afternoon, city council adjourned its meeting, the city band and fire brigade led a parade of hundreds to the station and the mayor arrived in Vancouver's only horse-drawn cab to meet the train at the Canadian Pacific Railway station at the foot of Howe Street.

The little station served Vancouver for the next twelve years. When its replacement was finished, the CPR hauled the station down the tracks to the foot of Heatley Avenue and handed it over to William Alberts, one of the original CPR switchmen. Alberts was involved in a workplace accident in the late 1890s. He lived in the station rent-free for the rest of his life, which proved to be quite long—he died in 1948 at the age of eighty.

Alberts and his wife, Isabella, raised their three children at their station house. When their daughter Irene and her husband, Noel Ross, returned the house to the CPR after her father's death, a *Vancouver Sun* reporter and photographer were there to record it. The reporter noted "the moss-covered roof" and the "goodbye" that had been scribbled on the floor of the former waiting room, which still had the original benches and stove, as well as the former garden that had been consumed by railway tracks. Irene told him she'd watched the troop trains come and go during both world wars and said that she was so used to train whistles and bells that she never even heard them.[2]

The arrival of the first train to Vancouver at the first CPR station at the foot of Howe Street—a simple two-storey, red wooden structure.
Vancouver Archives LGN 465, May 23, 1887

THE SECOND CPR STATION

The second CPR station didn't make it to its fifteenth birthday. It's shown here being demolished after the current and third CPR station was completed in July 1914.

Vancouver Archives 152-1.065

Even if you don't love the architecture—and I do happen to be a fan of anything that's gothic and grim and wears a turret—you've got to admit that the second CPR station would have made an amazing addition to our current urban landscape. Designed by Edward Maxwell in the railway's early Château style, the station dominated the foot of Granville Street with its two massive turrets and an arched entranceway made from Calgary limestone.

But all this gorgeousness didn't save the building. It quickly became too small for a burgeoning Vancouver and was demolished in August 1914 and replaced by the current Waterfront Station.

LOTS FOR SALE IN SHAUGHNESSY HEIGHTS

In 1909, hundreds of Vancouver's richest citizens lined up on both sides of Granville Street and for more than four blocks along West Hastings Street to buy lots in Shaughnessy Heights—which just goes to show that real estate speculation has always been a Vancouver sport. As a condition of sale, all homes had to cost a minimum of $6,000—six times the price of an average house at the time.

Shopping for real estate Vancouver-style in 1909.
Vancouver Archives 677-526

FRANCIS RATTENBURY (1867-1935)

Francis Rattenbury had just turned twenty-five when he moved to Vancouver from England in 1892 and won a design competition for BC's Parliament Buildings against sixty seasoned architects. Rattenbury's climb to fame, and subsequent fall from grace, is well documented, but it's worth telling again, if only because it's a great story.

After his win, Rattenbury quickly filled his portfolio with a slew of residential and commercial buildings. These included Victoria's Empress Hotel, an extension to the first Hotel Vancouver and the Vancouver courthouse (now the Vancouver Art Gallery), which was, for a time, wedged between the second and third Hotel Vancouvers. He married Florence Nunn in 1898, had a couple of kids, and was the architect for both the CPR and the competing Grand Trunk Pacific Railway. Then in 1906 things started to unravel.

Rattenbury fell out with the CPR and resigned as their architect. He was now fully committed to the Grand Trunk and invested heavily in land around the proposed western terminus at Prince Rupert. But when railway boss Charles Melville Hays went down with the *Titanic* in 1912, so did most of Rattenbury's fortune. By 1918, the railway was bankrupt and the plans for Prince Rupert never materialized. In 1923, Rattenbury met Alma Pakenham. She was twice-married and thirty years his junior. They scandalized Victoria society and humiliated poor Florrie by flaunting their affair. The couple moved to Bournemouth, England, where Rattenbury should have been able to live out his life in obscurity—but the still beautiful Pakenham seduced George Stoner, their eighteen-year-old chauffeur.

In a fit of jealously, Stoner bludgeoned Rattenbury to death in 1935. Both Pakenham and Stoner were tried for murder. Pakenham was acquitted, but after hearing Stoner would hang, she promptly stabbed herself, threw herself into a river and drowned. Stoner later had his death sentence overturned and served just seven years in prison. He married in 1944, spent the rest of his life in Bournemouth and died in 2000 at eighty-three.

THE FIRST HOTEL VANCOUVER

Vancouver, VANCOUVER, B.C.

The sixty-room Hotel Vancouver opened on the corner of Granville and Georgia Streets in 1887. Eight years later, the CPR hired Francis Rattenbury to design a new hotel in the Château style. In the end, a scaled-down version was tacked onto the existing building. Other additions followed, until the CPR brought in New York architect Francis Swales to build a new hotel on the same site. The challenge: Swales had to incorporate the additions into the new hotel and to design it such that the hotel wouldn't be closed even for a day.

THE SECOND HOTEL VANCOUVER

The second Hotel Vancouver opened in 1916, lasted just thirty-three years and was the most elegant and ornate building that we ever destroyed. It had sixteen storeys at its highest point and was designed in the grand Italian Renaissance style. The CPR-owned hotel had a 100-foot-long (30.5-metre) bar that it claimed was the largest in Canada. It also contained a barbershop with sixteen chairs. There was a staff of more than 500 to run the whole place. Its exterior was dressed up with terracotta gargoyles, buffalo heads, carved antlered elk heads and larger-than-life moose. It had turrets and a trellised rooftop cafe and looked a bit like a giant wedding cake carved out of stone.

The hotel's guest list read like a who's who of celebrities of the day: Charlie Chaplin, Rudyard Kipling, Sarah Bernhardt, Sergei Rachmaninoff, Maurice Ravel, Anna Pavlova, John Barrymore, Edgar Rice Burroughs (creator of *Tarzan*), Mary Pickford and Douglas Fairbanks Senior. Sports stars Jack Dempsey and Babe Ruth stayed, and even Winston Churchill once hung his hat there. Then the stock market crashed, the Depression hit and the CPR's archrival, the Canadian National Railway, ran out of funds to finish its new hotel on the corner of Georgia and Burrard Streets. It sat there like a sad lump of steel honeycomb for several years, until the CPR, also hurting from the Depression, agreed to pitch in and help finish the hotel. In 1939, on their royal tour of Canada, King George VI and Queen Elizabeth opened the third Hotel Vancouver, where they stayed in suites on the fourteenth floor.

Rooftop garden at the second Hotel Vancouver.
Vancouver Archives PAN N120A, July 1916

Before the war, members of the public had unsuccessfully tried to repurpose the hotel as, variously, an auditorium, a museum and library, or a provincial government office building. But the public weren't aware that included in the deal between the CPR and CN was the proviso that as soon as the third Hotel Vancouver was finished, the exquisite second Hotel Vancouver would be torn down.

Then the Second World War got in the way and the hotel was leased to the Department of National Defence first as a recruiting centre and later for offices and barracks. In January 1946, thirty Canadian veterans, frustrated with the shortage of housing in Vancouver, seized the hotel. The occupying force hung a huge banner on the hotel's Granville Street wall that read "Action at Last/Veterans! Rooms for You. Come and Get Them." By the following week, 1,400 people had registered, and the hotel became a hostel for the formerly homeless veterans and their families.[3]

When the T. Eaton Company bought the hotel in 1948 there were 1,001 residents—304 of which were children. Most of the families were allocated affordable rental housing at the Renfrew Heights subdivision near Boundary Road and East Twenty-second Avenue or placed in converted huts at the Seaforth Armoury at Burrard Street near First Avenue. But the 219 single men and women were out on their own. From the old hotel, some furniture and carpets went to the new hotel, more to private homes; some paintings went to the CPR station, and the clock found a home in the Board of Trade offices inside the Marine Building.

Instead of building a ten-storey department store on the site of the second Hotel Vancouver, as was announced, Eaton's purchased Spencer's—at that time, BC's largest department store—and took over that store's space on West Hastings Street. The old hotel was so well built that it took ten months and nearly $1 million to demolish, and instead of providing much-needed rental housing, the site became a parking lot for the next two decades.

Mr and Mrs Norman Chapman and their three children became the first of the veterans and their families to occupy the Hotel Vancouver. They moved into Room 1024.

Province, *February 15, 1946*

BEHIND THE WALL AT THE HOTEL VANCOUVER

They were two of the first female sculptors in Canada, but Elza Mayhew and Beatrice Lennie have more in common than their gender and profession. They both created massive artworks that are now hidden behind walls in Vancouver buildings.

When Beatrice Lennie graduated from the first class at the Vancouver School of Decorative and Applied Arts (now Emily Carr University of Art + Design) in 1929, it took four piano movers to shift her diploma piece. She called it *Spirit of Mining*.

Lennie studied under Frederick Varley, J.W.G. Macdonald and Charles Marega. In 1975, she told a *Province* reporter that Marega had sculpted a Queen Anne ceiling for her family's Shaughnessy home on Matthews Avenue around 1910. "It was a large decorative oval with high relief of laurel. Our ceiling was much more beautiful

than Hycroft's or Alvo von Alvensleben's," she said. "I was just a little girl when our house was built but I can vaguely remember the ceiling all coming in pieces."[4]

Beatrice was the daughter of R.S. Lennie, a barrister who headed up the Lennie Commission—an inquiry into corruption in the Vancouver Police Department in 1928. Her wealthy family was horrified by her chosen career, and she received little emotional or financial support from them. "If I'd been a singer, they'd have sent me to Italy," she told the *Province*. "Sculpture was not respectable or lady-like. Singing was acceptable but a woman's place was in the home. There was terrible discrimination. Women had to be better than men. For one job I was on the scaffold at eight in the morning. I came down and just dropped in the evening. I had to prove something."[5]

Beatrice Lennie in front of the mural she designed for the Hotel Vancouver's lobby.

From First Class: Four Graduates from the Vancouver School of Decorative and Applied Arts, 1929, *courtesy Murray Maisey*

In 1939, CN commissioned Lennie to create a twelve-foot (3.7-metre) sculpture on the main floor of our current Hotel Vancouver. Called *Ascension*, the work was finished in blue steel, brass and chromium. But when the hotel renovated the lobby in 1967, Lennie's sculpture and two elevators were left on the wrong side of a new wall. "I used to think your sculpture would outlive you, but they boarded up one of mine," she said, eight years later. "They covered it with a wooden wall when they lowered the ceiling. It's discouraging in one's own lifetime."[6]

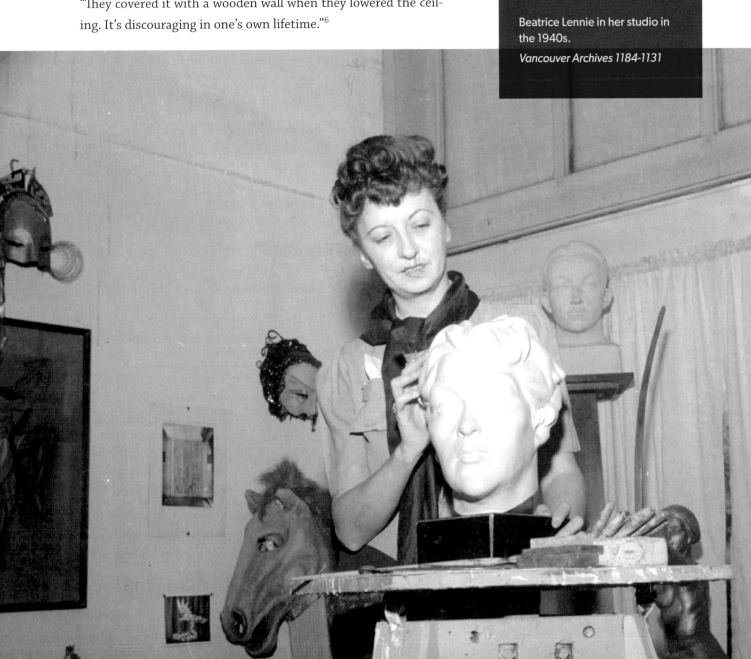

Beatrice Lennie in her studio in the 1940s.
Vancouver Archives 1184-1131

THE COVER-UP

900 West Hastings, designed by Thompson, Berwick and Pratt in 1965, was occupied by the Bank of Canada for thirty years.
Eve Lazarus photo, 2020

Elza Mayhew was already one of Canada's best-known sculptors, having represented the country at the Venice Biennale of 1964, when she was commissioned by the Bank of Canada to create a $30,000 sculpture for the lobby of their new building on West Hastings to mark the 1967 Canadian Centennial celebrations.

For almost two years, Mayhew worked on the sculpture in her studio in Victoria and in Eugene, Oregon, where she did her casting. She created a bronze wall-sized sculpture to represent the confidence and strength of the nation's central bank. It formed the whole end wall of the lobby. When it was unveiled, she said: "I wanted something that would go with the architecture and do something for the lobby. The work is abstract but is about people and where they live and go." It took six hours to move the sculpture into the bank lobby, and after it was installed, Elza said it "fitted like a glove."[7]

Fast-forward thirty years and 900 West Hastings Street sold to Canacemal, a Hong Kong–based investment firm that also inherited Mayhew's sculpture. Building manager Bart Slotman (who is now vice-president of Canacemal's Uptown Property Group) said one of the first things they wanted to do was renovate the lobby and "reposition it as a nice classy traditional office building" to attract new tenants and rid the space of its institutional bank feel. The sculpture, he says, didn't fit with the new design. "Art tends to provoke a reaction in people and most people thought it dark and sombre and depressing and it really wasn't suitable for the direction we wanted to take the building," he told me.

Elza Mayhew with her two-ton sculpture commissioned by the Bank of Canada in 1967.

Irene McAllister photo, courtesy Anne Mayhew

Elza's daughter, Anne Mayhew, says she tried to arrange a deal where Canacemal would donate the sculpture they'd inherited to the Art Gallery of Greater Victoria. There was an engineer and an architect on standby, and everything had been in place for months. "We were going to arrange and pay for the removal and transportation to Victoria," Anne told me. "The sculpture would be reassembled and stored at Elza's studio until all the paperwork was completed, and the gallery had the space prepared. Then, over a weekend, with no notice, the sculpture was boarded up."

Bart says that's simply not true. He says he spent about a year trying to donate the sculpture and had no takers. The main problem was the sculpture's size. Weighing in at more than two tons, it measured ten feet (three metres) tall by thirteen feet (four metres) long and was almost a three feet (one metre) thick in places. "It would have incurred quite a significant cost to move it. If you look at images of the building during construction, the building was finished around it."

Anne says the only time she has ever heard from Canacemal was in 2014, after she put the story of the "cover-up" on her website. Bart wrote to her saying that the sculpture was "intact, undisturbed, and well-protected," and the company would be willing to review the feasibility of relocating the artwork at a future renovation of the lobby.

"No one has proven that it's actually there," says Anne. "If it's not there, then somebody has melted it down."

Bart says: "We could have destroyed the sculpture, but we didn't. It's been left in place and we documented the hell out of it. Realistically that piece is going to sit there for the next twenty years and when I'm long retired and somebody else is renovating that lobby they are going to come across a pretty significant piece of art behind that wall."

Currently, sitting in front of the wall in the lobby is a driftwood piece Canacemal commissioned from North Vancouver artist Brent Comber. "I love Brent Comber's work. It has a very West Coast feel to it and we are getting a lot of positive feedback," says Bart.

STREETCAR ADVERTISING & THE HOBBY LOBBY RADIO SHOW

As the ad on the front of this streetcar attests, Dave Elman brought his US-based *Hobby Lobby* radio show to the stage of Vancouver's Beacon Theatre in 1944. A musician, songwriter, hypnotist and broadcaster, Elman came up with the idea in 1937 for a show in which people would "lobby for their hobby." Annette Weiss talked about her hobby of collecting puppy's teeth; for Loring W. Pratt it was collecting mammal, bird, fish and reptile skulls; R.B. Bilkowsky trained fishing worms (to do what I'm not sure); and Tanit Ikao hypnotized crocodiles. Elman's famous guests included Dale Carnegie, and First Lady Eleanor Roosevelt hosted the show when Elman was on holiday. The *Hobby Lobby* radio show ran until 1948.

No. 3 Davie Street at 600-block Granville Street in 1944.

Vancouver Archives
586-1872

VANCOUVER OPERA HOUSE

Vancouver Opera House, ca. 1899.

Vancouver Archives Bu N425

Once the CPR had a station and a hotel, the next step was to build the Vancouver Opera House. It was a beautiful building, with a lit-up dome-like roof, that opened in 1892 with 1,200 seats, a huge number considering the population of Vancouver at the time was just 13,000. The seats ranged from one dollar in the gallery to twenty dollars for a box that held up to six people. Although the theatre didn't host a lot of actual opera, it brought in such megastars as Sarah Bernhardt and Ethel Barrymore as well as a production of *Ben-Hur* that featured a cast of 275 and a chariot race with live horses.

Tim Sullivan and John Considine took over the Opera House in 1913, renamed it the Orpheum[8] and hosted the Orpheum Circuit Vaudeville. "Big" Tim Sullivan was a well-connected former New York politician and Considine had got his start

The drop screen with this Banff landscape was painted in New York and sent by rail to Vancouver on two flatcars, ca. 1891.

Vancouver Archives Bu P7

managing a seedy saloon in the rough part of Seattle before breaking in and championing more polite family vaudeville in the Pacific Northwest. Considine was notorious for shooting to death William Meredith, the former Seattle chief of police, in 1901. Considine and Meredith had a long-running dispute, and Considine was found not guilty after it was discovered that Meredith had fired the first two shots, one of which grazed Considine's head.[9] Later, this Orpheum hosted stars such as Jack Benny and the Marx Brothers. Over the years it went by a number of names, including Vancouver Theatre, the Lyric, the International Cinema and the Lyric again.

In May 1969, Joe McKinnon was interviewed for a story about "the Golden Age of Demolition." He had the contract to demolish all the buildings on Block 52 in downtown Vancouver, and he was showing off the five-ton wrecking ball that he'd bought in Seattle—the largest, he said, that had ever been used in Vancouver. "It smashed right through the balcony of the Lyric," he bragged, adding, "About ninety percent of a demolished building is just rubbish."[10]

And, just like that, the Lyric Theatre, Granville Mansions and York Hotel—all part of Block 52—were reduced to 500 loads of brick and wood to make way for Eaton's department store.

MOVIE PROJECTIONIST ESCAPES DEATH WHEN BOMB WRECKS CAR

On January 21, 1932, Wally Woolridge, a thirty-eight-year-old movie projectionist at the Colonial Theatre at Granville and Dunsmuir finished his shift at 7:30 p.m., got in his car, turned on his lights and was hurled twenty feet (six metres) in the air through the roof of his car. He landed on the gravel several feet away concussed, deafened and with blood pouring from both ears.

Packed with dynamite, the bomb was powerful enough to break windows in nearby buildings. Woolridge's life was spared because the bomb was placed at the back of the driver's seat and the backrest deflected the explosion. His heavy coat softened his fall.

"I think I know who did it. I could put my finger on the man if I wanted to," Woolridge told a reporter, adding that he wasn't going to name names. "I can tell you one thing, though. It's the work of racketeers. The thing tonight is just another episode in the story of bombings which have been taking place all over the continent during the last few months."[11]

Clearly, you had to be pretty brave to see a movie in the 1930s.

Woolridge was an active member of the BC Projectionists' Society, which was affiliated with the American Federation of Labor. According to newspapers, the "recognized group" was caught up in a war with "the rebels," a breakaway group of non-union employees. The attempt on Woolridge's life followed a spate of stink bombs that previously found their way to the non-union Royal Theatre (formerly the Pantages Theatre on West Hastings).

This was the third attempt on Woolridge's life. A year before, he was the victim of another failed car bombing while driving along Hastings Street, and just weeks later, shots were fired at him as he came home from work late one night. Either the murderers were completely incompetent or Woolridge was just very lucky.

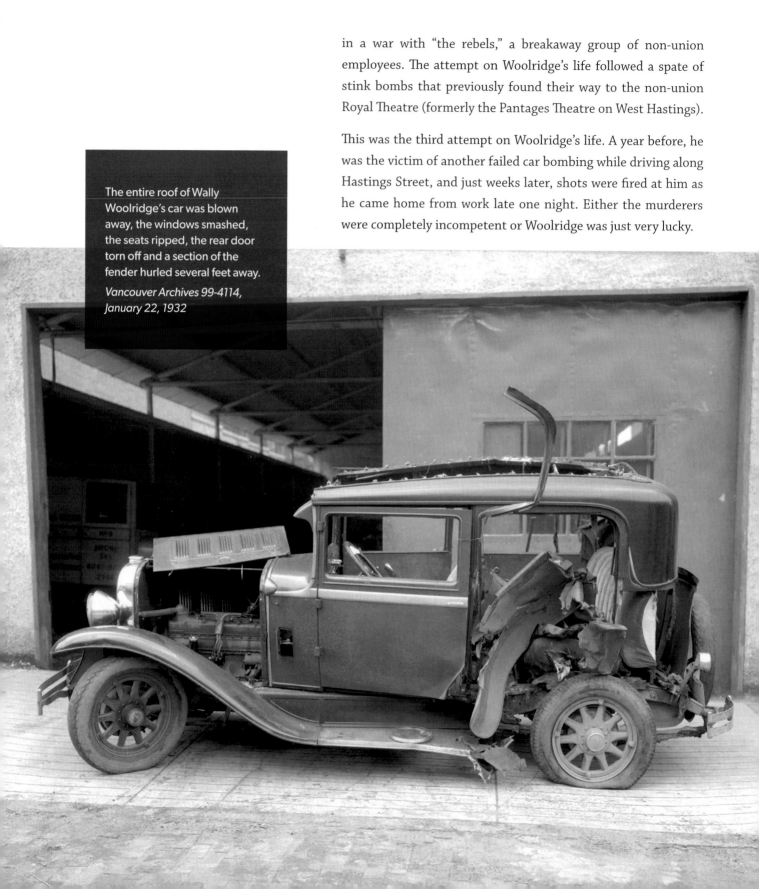

The entire roof of Wally Woolridge's car was blown away, the windows smashed, the seats ripped, the rear door torn off and a section of the fender hurled several feet away.

Vancouver Archives 99-4114, January 22, 1932

MISS MOLLISON'S GLENCOE LODGE

The Glencoe Lodge opened at the corner of West Georgia and Burrard Streets in 1906. Sugar baron Benjamin Tingley Rogers owned it. He had bought two houses, raised them, added two storeys and turned the combined building into a boutique hotel, operated by the fabulous Miss Jean Mollison.

Jean's older sister, Annie, came to Canada from Scotland in 1888, armed with an introduction to the head of the CPR. Still in her early twenties, Annie became the first manager of the railway's new Banff Springs Hotel. Jean became her assistant. It wasn't long before Jean was sent to manage Fraser Canyon House at North Bend, BC, and later a chalet at Lake Louise, Alberta, while Annie opened hotels around BC at Field, Emerald Lake, Yoho and Glacier.

Under Jean's management, the CPR's small chalet at Lake Louise grew into a large hotel with 200 rooms. She told the *Province*: "The last two years I was there they would sometimes wire me from Calgary that there would be 1,500 people coming for lunch, many of them to stay the night and we had to rig up many curtains behind which the overflow could sleep."[12]

B.T. Rogers wanted Jean Mollison to run his hotel in Vancouver. To sweeten the deal, he threw in three months of free rent and $20,000 (about $570,000 in 2020) to spend on furnishing the hotel any way she wished. Jean named the hotel for the village she came from in Scotland. She often arranged and sang at concerts for the guests—some who lived there while their houses were being built and others who made it their permanent residence.

Historian and author Michael Kluckner says that after Rogers died in 1918, the operating revenue from the Glencoe was divided among his three daughters. The sugar refinery stock was given to his widow and sons. "The cash was a needed supplement for the two grown-up daughters, Mary and Elspeth, both of whom had married itinerant Russian musicians," he says.

Tom Roberts left a comment on my blog to tell me that his grandmother Agnes Strain arrived in Vancouver from Scotland in 1912 and worked as a housekeeper at the Glencoe. Her daughter Margaret, Tom's aunt, who, at age eleven, was known in the newspapers as the "wonder child," often accompanied Jean Mollison on her flute at recitals, when the little girl wasn't on the vaudeville circuit. Tom says his grandmother told him that Miss Mollison treated her like family and often gave her gifts. His family, he says, still has a set of cups and saucers with the Glencoe Lodge insignia.

By 1932, the Depression was in full swing. The previous year, the widowed Mrs Rogers had agreed to let Miss Mollison pay only half rent, but the Rogers daughters couldn't make ends meet. Miss Mollison lost the lease and the Glencoe became the Belfred Hotel but failed to rally under its new management, and the building was demolished that same year.

The site stood empty for a couple of years until Standard Oil took up the lease. The gas station with its distinctive Spanish tile roof was a fixture of that corner of Georgia and Burrard until 1969, when it was demolished to make way for the Royal Centre and the uninspiring Royal Bank building.

As for Jean Mollison, she promptly opened the New Glencoe Lodge at 2020 Barclay Street. It probably also struggled during the Depression, and she moved to smaller digs on Davie Street and started the Glencoe Coffee and Novelty Shop, where she specialized in her famous Glencoe ginger cake and traditional Scottish shortbread. She died in 1951, aged eighty-two.

BC's Mount Mollison is named for Jean and Annie.

TOP Glencoe Lodge interior.
Neil Whaley collection

MIDDLE The Standard Oil gas station replaced the Glencoe Lodge and remained there until 1969, when it was demolished to make way for the Royal Bank building.
Vancouver Archives 447-363, 1970

BOTTOM The northwest corner of Burrard and West Georgia has been home to the Royal Bank and office tower since 1973.
Eve Lazarus photo, 2020

Corner of Bedroom, Glencoe Lodge, Vancouver, B. C.

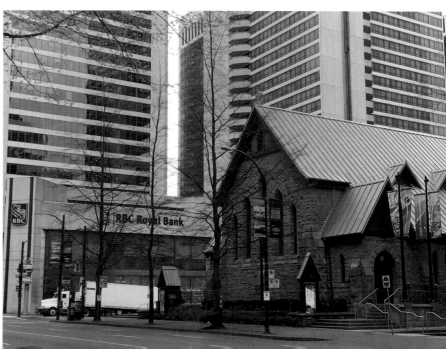

THE FIRST VANCOUVER ART GALLERY

You may not know his name but if you've spent any time in Vancouver, you will recognize his work. Italian-born Charles Marega is the sculptor who created the two concrete lions that stand guard at the south end of the Lions Gate Bridge. His other notable commissions include the nine topless terracotta maidens that populate the cornice of the Sun Tower on West Pender Street; the bronze bust of David Oppenheimer, Vancouver's second mayor, at the entrance to Stanley Park; the statue of Captain Vancouver in front of Vancouver City Hall; the statues of fourteen icons of BC history that line the Parliament Buildings in Victoria; and the drinking fountain that sits in Alexandra Park in honour of lifeguard Joe Fortes.

Marega won the commission to sculpt the heads of Michelangelo and Leonardo da Vinci that flanked the front door of the Vancouver Art Gallery—not the gallery that is currently housed in the imposing neoclassical former courthouse, but the first one, which was at 1145 West Georgia Street.

The original art gallery opened in 1931 in an Art Deco building, situated on Georgia Street a few blocks west from its current location, designed by the architecture firm Sharp and Thompson. George Sharp was a respected artist and a founding faculty

October 5, 1931, opening day of the first Vancouver Art Gallery, 1145 West Georgia Street.

Vancouver Archives 99-4062

member of the Vancouver School of Decorative and Applied Arts, and he designed the building to fit perfectly into the largely residential West End neighbourhood. It had a main hall, two large galleries and two smaller ones, as well as a sculpture hall, a lecture hall and a library. The gallery held a collection of fifty-eight oil paintings, twenty-four watercolours, two sculptures, nine drawings, twenty-three etchings and 178 reproductions. At the entrance, Marega carved the names of those who were considered great painters of the time (none were Canadian, and all were men).

After the Second World War, Group of Seven artist Lawren Harris raised $300,000 for the gallery, which resulted in the building expanding to three times its original size to accommodate the works of Emily Carr and some of Harris's own paintings. The Art Deco facade disappeared and Marega's sculptures were no longer considered appropriate for the new sleeker modern building. A classified ad ran in the *Province* on July 13, 1951: "Architectural sculpture by Charles Marega formerly on facade and foyer of Vancouver Art Gallery now for sale. Details given and bids accepted. Phone Curator, PA4845." In 1975, author Doreen (Peggy) Imredy, wife of sculptor Elek Imredy, said that if they didn't sell, the Vancouver Art Gallery planned to throw out the busts. Peggy claimed, "A workman said if they were throwing them out, he knew someone who would like them. I have seen them and they were well cared for and beautifully situated in a garden in the Lower Mainland." Imredy declined to say who bought them.[13]

In 1983, the Vancouver Art Gallery moved into its current digs at the old courthouse, taking with it $15 million in art. Two years later, the original building was demolished. Now the Trump International Hotel and Tower and the FortisBC Centre straddle its old space.

West Georgia Street was still heavily residential when this photo was taken in April 1931.
Vancouver Archives 99-3870

BC Centennial
Fountain, 1969.

*Vancouver Archives
780-62*

THE CENTENNIAL FOUNTAIN

In 1966, BC was preparing to celebrate the centennial of the colonial union of the mainland and Vancouver Island. In recognition of this, the province paid for a $45,000 fountain to be installed in front of the West Georgia Street entrance of the Vancouver courthouse, the building that would become the Vancouver Art Gallery in 1983. Installation of the fountain began in the spring, and because the province wanted to keep the design a secret until it was unveiled, Premier W.A.C. Bennett had the site surrounded by wooden hoardings. But instead of having the panels painted green and white, the colours of Bennett's Socred Party, as the provincial government had intended, Mayor Bill Rathie held a paint-in on April 6, 1966—Vancouver's eightieth birthday. The event was a huge success and included over 100 art students who had signed up and been assigned spots along the hoarding. The art stayed up until the fountain was revealed the following December.

The fountain, designed by landscape architect Robert Savery, featured a sixteen-foot (4.8-metre) marble sculpture and blue and green mosaic tiles crafted by artist Alex von Svoboda. It pumped out over 343,000 gallons (1.3 million litres) of water an hour.

LEFT The fountainless public space in front of the Vancouver Art Gallery in 2020.

Eve Lazarus photo

RIGHT The original fountain was created by Charles Marega in 1912. It now sits at the Hornby Street side of the building.

Eve Lazarus photo, 2020

Over the next forty-eight years, the fountain endured visits from canoeists, waders and pranksters with soapsuds. It was the meeting place and rallying point for dozens of public demonstrations, including Grey Cup rioters and anti-war protestors in the 1960s, 4/20 cannabis smoke-ins and the tent city of Occupy Vancouver in 2011.

In 2014, the fountain was removed. It had been turned off the year before after a leak was found in the art gallery's storage area which runs underneath the entire plaza. And although the public hasn't wholeheartedly embraced the new rather sterile-looking plaza, some people didn't embrace the fountain back when it was first revealed in 1966. At that time, the local artistic community was outraged by the bureaucratic unilateral decision regarding the design commission. Critics

felt the government should stay out of the fountain business and put all public art to a competition. "[Government] employees aren't qualified to design works of art or sculpture. They are incompetent in these fields of art," said Frank Low-Beer, chair of the Community Arts Council committee.[14]

They had a point, but I loved that fountain anyway.

The Centennial Fountain had replaced one that sculptor Charles Marega created in 1912. His fountain languished in storage until 1983. When the Vancouver Art Gallery moved into the building, Marega's fountain was installed on the Hornby Street side.

Who knows, maybe we'll also see a reappearance of the Centennial Fountain— or at least parts of it—sometime in the future.

RIGHT An artist puts finishing touches on a mural painted on the hoarding at the Vancouver Art Gallery building paint-in in April 1966.

Vancouver Archives 2009-001.193

BELOW Artists painting a mural on the hoarding at the Vancouver Art Gallery building in April 1966.

Vancouver Archives 2009-001.169

IN AND OUT OF VOGUE

While sleuthing through files at the Vancouver Art Gallery library, local blogger Jason Vanderhill found a photo of artists Jack Shadbolt and Paul Goranson painting a mural on one of the walls of the Vogue Theatre in 1940, the year before it opened. On separate occasions author Aaron Chapman and former Vogue manager Bill Allman have searched the building, and examined its plans and old photos, but if the mural still exists, it's very well hidden.

The construction of Vogue Theatre was financed by proceeds from the Prohibition-era rum-running ventures of Vancouver's Reifel family. Harry Reifel hired a Toronto architectural firm to design the Art Deco theatre in 1940. Inside, the auditorium ceiling was tiered and lined with incandescent lights to resemble coloured waves. When the theatre first opened, giant golden mermaids were painted on the walls, and the washrooms sported aquamarine and orange tiles.

Outside, the Vogue's distinctive neon sign is topped by a huge kneeling figure of the goddess Diana that looks suspiciously like a car's hood ornament. She's actually the second Diana; the first was commissioned by Reifel for $500 and made of sheet metal and covered in gold leaf by artist Bud Graves. When Odeon Theatres renovated the Vogue in the 1960s, the goddess was in rough shape and sent to the scrap heap. A distraught Reifel immediately commissioned a second statue at ten times the price. "The front of the theatre without her was like a Jersey cow without horns," he told a reporter at the time.[15] The sign—one of the largest along theatre row's sea of neon—has changed colours over the years and is now red and yellow. The Vogue Theatre was designated a national historic site in 1993.

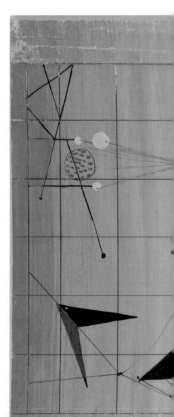

Bill Allman believes if the mural still exists it is behind the upper bar in the balcony lobby, which is now covered over with mirrors and panelling.

This wasn't the only Shadbolt mural lost to history. In 1959, the artist was commissioned to create *Pageant of Transformation in Nature*, for the restaurant of the Queen Elizabeth Theatre. It was wallpapered over in a renovation a few decades later, and when it came time to redecorate again in the mid-1990s, the mural was forgotten and the contractor demolished the entire wall, mural and all.

A Shadbolt mural called *Cycle of Seasons*, created for the Alcazar Hotel on Dunsmuir Street in 1949, managed to survive the hotel's 1982 demolition, but its present location remains a mystery. Angus McIntyre saved one of the standout green-and-red neon signs from the Alcazar Hotel and installed it inside his house.

ABOVE Jack Shadbolt, *Alcazar Mural Panel Study (study for Cycle of Seasons)*, 1949, gouache, graphite and ink on board, 29.4 × 18.1 cm. Collection of the Morris and Helen Belkin Art Gallery, University of British Columbia, gift of Jack & Doris Shadbolt, 1998.

Copyright © Simon Fraser University Galleries, Burnaby

THE ORILLIA

The Orillia at Robson and Seymour was just a memory by the time I moved to Vancouver in the mid-1980s, but from time to time I see a mention or a photo of this early mixed-use structure. One particularly poignant photo was taken just before its destruction in the 1980s and shows the Orillia boarded up, covered in music handbills, smeared with graffiti, and the words "Save Me!" scrawled across one of the plywood hoardings.

When I posted a story about the Orillia on my blog, it got an immediate response from people who had spent time there. Author and historian Michael Kluckner tells me he used to play pool there in the 1960s and that it was well known for Sid Beech's Vancouver Tamale Parlor, which operated there for decades as a popular dining and late-night hangout. Beech's eclectic menu ranged from tamales and enchiladas to Chinese noodles, spaghetti, soup and sandwiches.

Over the years there were rumours of a brothel that had set up shop in the Orillia. It was Funland Arcade, for a time, and Twiggy's, a gay disco. Twiggy's morphed into Faces in the 1970s.

RIGHT Menu from Sid Beech's Vancouver Tamale Parlor, 1937.

Tom Carter collection

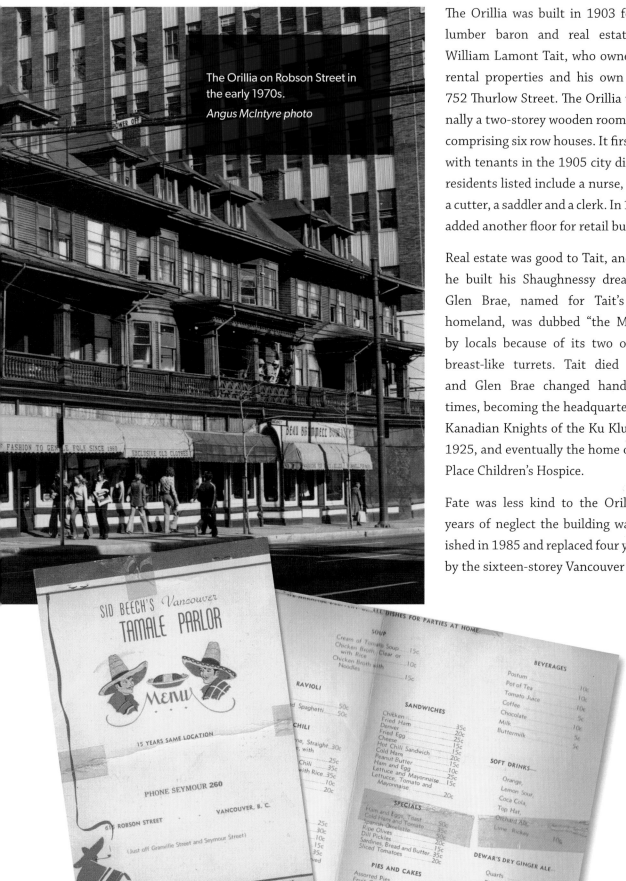

The Orillia on Robson Street in the early 1970s.
Angus McIntyre photo

The Orillia was built in 1903 for retired lumber baron and real estate tycoon William Lamont Tait, who owned several rental properties and his own house at 752 Thurlow Street. The Orillia was originally a two-storey wooden rooming house comprising six row houses. It first appears with tenants in the 1905 city directory—residents listed include a nurse, a painter, a cutter, a saddler and a clerk. In 1909, Tait added another floor for retail businesses.

Real estate was good to Tait, and in 1911 he built his Shaughnessy dream home. Glen Brae, named for Tait's Scottish homeland, was dubbed "the Mae West" by locals because of its two outlandish breast-like turrets. Tait died in 1919, and Glen Brae changed hands several times, becoming the headquarters for the Kanadian Knights of the Ku Klux Klan in 1925, and eventually the home of Canuck Place Children's Hospice.

Fate was less kind to the Orillia. After years of neglect the building was demolished in 1985 and replaced four years later by the sixteen-storey Vancouver Tower.

THE STOCK EXCHANGE

In 1929, the Vancouver Stock Exchange built an eleven-storey neo-Gothic tower on Howe Street as a monument to penny stocks and venture capital. The building featured marble and terrazzo floors, walls and ceilings, and an exterior finished with a polished granite base with terracotta for the first two and upper three storeys. It opened in June of that year, four months before the stock market crash and the onset of the Great Depression.

Founded in 1907, the VSE was basically a legal gambling operation that used a trading floor to raise money for risky enterprises and speculative stocks, which rarely turned a profit for investors but did attract a host of nefarious characters over the nine decades it was in business.

The VSE moved to 540 Howe Street in 1947, and in 1981 moved to a tower a few blocks away to the Pacific Centre. Although it was now on Granville Street, the VSE was still referred to as "Howe Street."

I joined the VSE public relations department in 1987, the same year that David Cruise and Alison Griffiths published *Fleecing the Lamb: The Inside Story of the Vancouver Stock Exchange*. My job was to get the new visitors' centre up and running so investors could check their stock prices and hapless school children could learn about penny stocks. I was still there in 1989, when a cover story in *Forbes* magazine famously called the VSE the "scam capital of the world." I quit soon afterward, went to journalism school and got hired as a business reporter at the *Vancouver Sun*. Market manipulations and various swindles continued into the late 1990s, until the VSE merged with the Alberta Stock Exchange and soon after disappeared inside the Toronto Stock Exchange.

TOP Vancouver Stock Exchange trading floor, June 29, 1979.
Vancouver Sun, *George Diack photo*

BOTTOM EXchange Hotel, 2019.
Courtesy EXchange Hotel Vancouver

Meanwhile, the VSE's former headquarters on Howe Street was sitting on a prime piece of real estate that was zoned for a much higher building than the existing eleven-storey one. The heritage preservation community braced for a demolition order. But instead of knocking the building down, Credit Suisse stepped in with Harry Gugger, the starchitect behind the restoration of London's Tate Modern Extension, to incorporate the old building into a new design. In this case, keeping the facade is a real win for heritage preservation in development-hungry Vancouver, and a nod to the original architects— Townley and Matheson, the same firm that designed Vancouver City Hall.

The VSE's old digs is now the EXchange, a luxury hotel that opened in 2019. The new building is an office tower with retail space on the ground floor. Except for the facade and the lobby and some of the ground floor, most of the structure has been gutted.

One of my favourite parts of working for the VSE was heading to the trading floor to watch the board boys write up the trades and then watch the floor traders throw the white chits of buy-and-sell orders up in the air at the day's close. So I was excited to see that the trading floor has been re-created inside a bar in the EXchange Hotel called the Open Outcry. An old tickertape machine, archival photos and a huge mural add some authenticity to the place.

THE EVOLUTION OF WEST PENDER & HOWE STREETS: BEFORE THE STOCK EXCHANGE BUILDING

ABOVE 1899–1913: Alhambra Theatre, Theatre Royal, the People's Theatre and the first Orpheum.

Vancouver Archives Bu N424, ca. 1899

RIGHT 1914–27: The building that took the theatre's place hosted a variety of different businesses including a tire dealership, a taxi company and Sing Lung Laundry.

Vancouver Archives 99-689, 1918

Cathedral Place has fibreglass versions of the original nurses as a nod to the building's history.

Eve Lazarus photo, 2020

FINDING THE RHEA SISTERS

Do you remember the Rhea sisters? They were three eleven-foot (3.4-metre) terracotta statues of First World War nurses that guarded the tenth floor of the Georgia Medical-Dental Building on West Georgia. Both the GM-DB and the still-standing Marine Building were important Art Deco buildings designed by McCarter Nairne architects within a few years of each other. Nina Rumen of the BC History of Nursing Society says John Young McCarter and George Colvil Nairne both served overseas during the First World War. McCarter was seriously wounded and credited nurses for saving his life. The sculptures were their way of honouring nurses.

The GM-DB, our first Art Deco skyscraper, came down in 1989; it was just sixty-two, not even old enough to be considered a senior citizen. But although the building is a distant memory, the nurses are still around—just in different parts of the city.

I thought I found one when I was driving along East Hastings Street in Burnaby, in the retail yard of Ital Decor. Mario Tinucci, president of the building ornamentations company, told me that the statue is a fibreglass version that he cast from an original nurse statue in 1990. It was the first of four that were replicated—the other three replicas are attached to Cathedral Place, the tower

designed by Paul Merrick that replaced the GM-DB. Paul was the architect behind the restoration of several heritage buildings in the city including the Marine Building, the Orpheum Theatre and the conversion of the BC Hydro Building into residences. But instead of a do-over, the GM-DB received a demolition order and Paul was charged with replacing it. Now I like Cathedral Place. It's nicely tiered, the roof fits in with the Hotel Vancouver across the street and, besides the nurses, it even has a few gargoyles and lions pasted about as a reminder of its predecessor. It's easy to appreciate Paul's skill in the monastery-like courtyard that joins Cathedral Place to Christ Church Cathedral and the Bill Reid Gallery.

When I interviewed Paul in 2014 we talked about some of the heritage buildings that he'd restored. I asked him how it was decided whether to restore a building or pull it down and start from scratch.

"The focus of architecture is to make a building," Paul told me. "And when it's all said and done, buildings need to be objects of utility, to serve the people's uses and needs inside them. They are there to provide shelter, but they are also hopefully concerned with affording delight with the experience. This keeps coming back to your question—what is heritage? How precious should we be about it—and to use your phrase—should we mess with

CATHEDRAL PLACE
VANCOUVER, CANADA

ARCHITECT: PAUL MERRICK
DESIGN TEAM: MICHAEL HUGGINS, DAVID WONG, RAY PRADINUK

it? If you choose not to you better have good reason and if you choose to you better have good reason. I always thought if you could make pieces of the city—which is all a building is, just another piece of the city—if we can make an environment that we're happy to leave to our descendants, then that's as good as you can do."

Architect's rendering
of Cathedral Place.

Courtesy David Wong

The original three nurse sculptures were affectionately called the Rhea sisters—Gono, Pyor and Dia—by patients of the medical building but they were in rough shape by the late 1980s, and the cost to restore them was upwards of $70,000 each. Instead, Cathedral Place developer Ron Shon donated them to the Vancouver Heritage Foundation. He also donated some of the terracotta animals, spandrel panels and chevron mouldings from the main entrance, and the secondary arch, which is now a fixture inside the Bill Reid Gallery.

The VHF donated one of the nurses to the Museum of Vancouver in 2000 and later sold the other two original nurses to Discovery Parks at UBC. Wendy Nichols, curator of collections at the museum, says their nurse resides at UBC on a long-term loan, and now all three of the original nurses are attached to the university's Technology Enterprise Facility III building. This is rather odd, since the building was completed in 2003 and, according to Nan Martin at the BC History of Nursing Society, has no connection to either nursing or the First World War.

If you'd like a close-up look, a plaster version of one of the nurse's heads is in the lobby of Cathedral Place.

THE DEVONSHIRE (1924-81)

The Devonshire Hotel
on West Georgia in
1976.

*Vancouver Archives
780-30*

The Devonshire Hotel, which sat between the Georgia Hotel and the Georgia Medical-Dental Building, was originally designed as an apartment building but by the 1930s, it was a hotel. I never saw the Devonshire, but I love one of its stories.

According to newspaper reports, after being kicked out of the racist Hotel Vancouver in 1951, Louis Armstrong and his All Stars walked across the street and were immediately given rooms in the Devonshire. Supposedly, Duke Ellington, Lena Horne and the Mills Brothers wouldn't stay anywhere else.

Former *Globe and Mail* reporter and author Rod Mickleburgh was there when the Devonshire was demolished. "I thought the loss of the Dev was awful. The Dev was the poor cousin of the Hotel Georgia, an old-fashioned pile-of-bricks hotel in a great location right downtown," he says. "I loved the corned beef sandwiches and glass of beer I'd get in their beer parlour, served, of course, by waiters in red jackets on small, round, terry cloth–covered tables. A glass of beer was twenty cents—you gave the unionized waiter a quarter."

THE OLDEST BUILDING IN VANCOUVER

Frank Holt lived next to the Marine Building for sixteen years—and his little house predated it by many more. In 1945, Vancouver Breweries Limited ran an ad in the *Vancouver Sun* as part of a wartime series encouraging people to buy bonds or war savings stamps. The ad asked, "Do you know Vancouver?" and showed a 1935 photo by W.J. Moore of the Marine Building, the Quadra Club and a circle around Holt's place, which was described as "the Oldest Building in Vancouver."

Holt came to Vancouver on the first transcontinental train in 1887 and was one of the founders of Christ Church Cathedral. He lived as a squatter in his one-room house, which, after 1930, huddled in the shadow of the Marine Building. Holt and his cabin have long been lost to history, but it's a fascinating story, even if it does come from an ad.

According to the ad copy, CPR land commissioner Lauchlan Hamilton used the house when he was surveying Vancouver in 1885. "Clearing a space in the blackberry tangle, he drove his first stake where now is the corner of Hamilton Street and Victory Square. From this stake, his men cut a peep-hole through the forest along the dirt trail that led to Spratt's Oilery. Using the old cottage as a mark, Hamilton set the lines of our present Hastings Street, on which the street system of Vancouver is based."[16] There used to be a plaque at Hamilton and Hastings explaining this early bit of town planning.

The house was built in 1875 as a bunkhouse mess hall for the workers of Spratt's Oilery, a company that processed herring for fish oil. The house outlasted the oilery and survived the Great Vancouver Fire of 1886, and in 1894, Holt moved in. When

When the Marine Building first opened, four of its twenty-two floors were built into the cliff above the CPR's tracks.
Vancouver Archives Bu N7, 1935

Holt found out that four of the rooms were taxable because they were on city property, he tore them down and stayed in the one-room shack.

When John Buchan* (Baron Tweedsmuir) visited Vancouver as Governor General of Canada in the late 1930s, his attention was called to this shabby little relic of our past. "'I hope the people of Vancouver will preserve it!' he exclaimed, fervently," went the ad.

Well, no sir, we did not.

Holt was still living in the house in 1943, when the foundations started to give way and the front porch fell down the embankment. Holt, who was ninety at the time, helped workers install a new foundation. Then, in 1946, a fire broke out and trapped Holt in the house. Miraculously, firefighters found him in the debris and carried him to safety. The house was not so lucky and, in the end, neither was Holt. He died in December 1946, less than two months after his home burned down.

*Fun fact: Buchan wrote the novel *The Thirty-Nine Steps*, which was adapted into the classic Alfred Hitchcock movie.

Frank Holt's cabin, ca. 1932.
Vancouver Archives Bu N16

THE DEATH OF SEATON STREET

Until 1915, the address of Frank Holt's cabin was 1003 Seaton Street. Seaton Street was the part of West Hastings Street that ran from Burrard to Jervis. The street was dubbed "Blueblood Alley" after its wealthy occupants, which included Mayor Thomas Townley, prominent businessman Henry Ogle Bell-Irving and Vancouver's first solicitor, Alfred St. George Hamersley. In the early twentieth century, the bluebloods began to leave the alley for higher ground above English Bay, and by 1915, the name, just like the rich, had disappeared.

RIGHT Bryan Adams outside the Marine Building, 1989.

Robert Karpa photo

BELOW The Bank of Montreal opened a branch at 586 Granville in 1893. The bank moved out in 1925 and the Imperial Bank of Canada (shown here in 1955) moved in and stayed for the next thirty years. It was demolished in 1958 and replaced by the building that currently stands there.

Vancouver Archives 447-333

IMPERIAL BANK OF CANADA/ CIBC

B.C. BINNING'S SECRET MURAL

The Imperial Bank's six-storey replacement at 586 Granville Street featured a mid-century modern design, including terrazzo floors, polished granite and marble columns.

Eve Lazarus photo, 2020

Next time you're downtown and have a mascara emergency or need some aspirin, drop into the Shoppers Drug Mart at Granville and Dunsmuir. Once you hit the cosmetics area, you might just forget what you came in there for, because opposite the front entrance and right above the gift cards is one of the hidden wonders of Vancouver—a stunning ceramic tile mosaic created by legendary artist B.C. Binning in 1958.

Although it's probably best not to, if you go up to the second floor, you can actually touch one of the 200,000 pieces of Venetian glass that make up this massive mural that dominates the entire length of the wall. Binning, an artist who taught architecture, was commissioned by the Imperial Bank of Canada to celebrate the province's booming resource-based economy, from hydroelectricity and forestry to shipping and agriculture, in a mural made up of seventeen panel illustrations that came with a "key" to help interpret it. Binning spent more than three months in Venice overseeing its preparation, climbing a ladder a few times each day to look down at the growing tile and marble mosaic for the overall effect. When the greens weren't as vibrant as he expected, he had the tiles changed. When the mosaic was finished—all 500 square feet (fifty square metres) of it—it was shipped to Canada in twelve boxes, to be reassembled on the wall like a giant jigsaw puzzle.

B.C. Binning's mural at Shoppers Drug Mart on Granville and Dunsmuir.

Eve Lazarus photo, 2020

THE ESTABLISHMENT

Painter Jack Shadbolt loved B.C. Binning's mural on Granville Street so much, he wrote a letter to the editor of the *Vancouver Sun* in March 1958 to praise it— in contrast to Paul Huba's tiled ceramic in the new post office on West Georgia Street, which Shadbolt thought was a "public disgrace." In a letter, Shadbolt writes of Huba's work: "The sculptured figure fails by its tepid ineptitude at understanding the possibilities of low relief and by its uninspired banality. The inside ceramic panel, on the contrary, is sheer, inspired banality. Who could have conceived a more wonderful travesty of present postal service symbolism than the pre-Raphaelite lady in the flowing Greek gown sending her fateful letter off through her cupid boy into the blue, blue yonder? How sweetly, touchingly, tenderly bilge-like!"[17]

Yikes!

Possibly, this aversion to Huba's sculptures had more to do with the two artists themselves than with their creations. Both Shadbolt and Binning taught at the Vancouver School of Art and worked with the establishment at the time. Huba worked in a studio in Kitsilano surrounded by other renegade artists and sculptors such as Frank Molnar, George Fertig and Jock Hearn who were mostly shunned by the hierarchy then at the Vancouver Art Gallery.

LETTER TO THE EDITOR

Vancouver Sun

May 7, 1958

Since I was so openly critical concerning the sculpture and the main lobby ceramic mural in the new post office, perhaps you would be good enough to publish this letter of praise of something.

I think the main lobby of the new Imperial Bank building is nothing short of tremendous in its space concept, the beauty of its fittings and, above all, in its bold and imaginative conception of the true function of a mural.

This mural completely spanning the upper space of the end wall, gorgeous in surface and telling its message in simple pictographs is a great achievement. That BC Binning is a consummate architectural decorator goes without saying: but here is a new Binning in magnificent Venetian mosaic, a masterpiece in Canadian or any other terms and an exciting example of inspired coordination between architect and artist.

And guess who did this building? I am told—and I am most happy to acknowledge, the same architect who did the post office.

Jack Shadbolt
461 N. Glynde

PAUL HUBA AND THE CANADA POST BUILDING

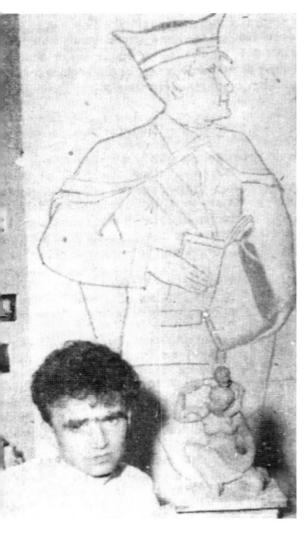

Paul Huba.

Province, September 15, 1956

When the main post office was built on West Georgia Street in the 1950s, it was the largest welded steel structure in the world. It was essentially a five-storey machine that covered an entire city block, wrapped in an International Style exterior and capped with a rooftop helipad—which was used all of twice before someone did the math and figured out that delivering mail by helicopter from the post office to Vancouver International Airport wasn't a viable option.

Despite what artist Jack Shadbolt felt, I'm a huge fan of the building and its art: two identical coats of arms made from cast aluminum on the front of the building and a sixteen-foot (five-metre) postman cut into Swedish red granite adjacent to the Homer Street entrance—all the work of Paul Huba. Inside hung a mural by Orville Fisher depicting the evolution of mail delivery. Shadbolt liked Fisher's work, but said in the letter to the editor that he felt he couldn't praise it because Fisher was a colleague at the Vancouver School of Art and he didn't want to be seen as part of a clique protecting their own vested interests!

Another of Huba's pieces took up a chunk of the wall inside the southeast corner of the building. The ceramic of a woman and child originally overlooked a large retail area. It was highly visible

Canada Post building, ca. 1960.
Neil Whaley collection

OPPOSITE PAGE TOP
Paul Huba's ceramic.
*Cheryle Harrison,
Conserv-Arte*

**OPPOSITE PAGE
BOTTOM**
The letter.
*Cheryle Harrison,
Conserv-Arte*

to anyone riding up the escalator to the mezzanine level. Former operations manager Andrew Langdon tells me that over the years the retail area shrank as small postal outlets opened up in places like Shoppers Drug Mart. Walls went up to repurpose the space and the mural was hidden from public view.

For decades, says Andrew, the only people who could see the mural were three or four employees who worked in the restricted area. "I was amazed when I saw it for the first time in the nineties. It was at least twelve feet [3.7 metres] high," he says. "It was almost as big as the whole room itself."

After I wrote about the mural on my blog, Blair Mercer told me that his mother, Beatrice Mary Hayes, was the model for the woman in the ceramic. Beatrice told Blair an architect approached her at a party in Shaughnessy in the early 1950s. The architect was apparently quite taken with Beatrice, who was a buyer for Hudson's Bay, and told her that he had commissioned an artist to do a ceramic for the new post office. He asked her if she would be willing to sit for him. Blair remembers his mother first taking him to the post office to see the ceramic when he was about ten.

There isn't much known about the Hungarian-born Paul Huba, possibly because he only lived in Vancouver for five years. I did find out that Huba moved to Vancouver in 1954 and three years later brought out his English wife, Sybil, and two sons, Dezso, fifteen, and Mark, seventeen, from England.

I tracked Dezso down at his home in Ashcroft, BC. Dezso says his father was in a relationship with a medical doctor named Ailsa Thurgar, and when he and his brother and mother arrived, his father installed his mistress in a room behind his studio and moved his family into the apartment above. Dezso says his mother tolerated the situation. "She didn't like having a second woman, but she couldn't do anything about it," he says. Ailsa and his mother were "civil" when they encountered each other, says Dezso. Huba died in 1959 from asthma and emphysema at age forty-six. Ailsa attended Huba's funeral, and she and Dezso remained close friends until her death in 1999.

In the 1950s and '60s, Kitsilano was filled with artists. Painter Jack Akroyd lived next door to the Hubas, and sculptor Elek Imredy was next door to him. Other artists who lived in the apartment building or nearby included Frank Molnar, Jack Dale, Jock Hearn, George Fertig and Roy Kiyooka, as well as poets John Newlove, Judith Copithorne and bill bissett.

When I profiled Molnar in 2009, he told me that Imredy had hired him and Akroyd to help with *Girl in a Wetsuit*—the sculpture that sits on a rock in the water off Stanley Park. Copithorne was one of three women who modelled for "the girl," and Dezso says his father hired George Norris (famous for the crab sculpture outside the Museum of Vancouver) and highly regarded sculptor David Marshall for fifty cents an hour to help make, glaze and then install the ceramic tiles at the Canada Post building.

Beatrice Mary Hayes, early 1950s.
Courtesy Blair Mercer

Huba had David Lambert, a writer and ceramic engineer, install a kiln in his Kitsilano studio and supply the glazes, says Dezso, who would hang out in his father's studio when he wasn't at school. "The tiles were about half an inch thick and made by hand," he says. "Once we fired them, my father would paint each tile individually. There were hundreds of tiles and sometimes the colours didn't come out right after you fired them. All of a sudden you'd have fifty wrecked tiles and you'd have to do them again."

I dropped by Huba's former studio and apartment in July 2019. John Taylor, an artist, photographer and set designer, has lived there since 1988 and kindly gave me a tour. Although Taylor didn't know of Huba, he knew Elek Imredy well. There's a photo that Taylor took of Imredy in his old studio window in 1990, four years before he died.

Cheryle Harrison, a professional art conservator, was brought in to preserve and safely remove the twelve-foot (3.66-metre) by twenty-foot (6.1-metre) mural from its wall at the former post office building. "There are 264 hand-glazed tiles that together weigh about 840 kilos [1,850 pounds], and these tiles were attached to a concrete block wall with mortar," she says. Tiles were broken when the mural was originally installed, and others cracked as the building shifted over the years. "Sometimes it was like working almost blind because the fine crack lines were not visible until the tile was near to coming off. Many times, I held my breath and worked quickly to save a damaged tile," says Cheryle. The tiles, each measuring a little less than ten inches (twenty-five centimetres) square, were then packed in more than sixty boxes to wait until the mural can be reassembled and installed in the new mixed-use building, called The Post, along with a few thousand Amazon employees, when it's finished around 2023.

RIGHT In the summer of 1997, Canada Post staffers painted a true-to-scale flag stamp that measured 98 feet by 115 feet (thirty metres by thirty-five metres), or roughly the size of a ten-storey building, on the roof of the Canada Post building. The roof mural raised $3,500 for Canuck Place Children's Hospice and was made into a forty-five-cent postage stamp the following February.

Vancouver Sun, *Glenn Baglo photo*

BELOW Aerial photo by the *Vancouver Sun*'s Bill Dennett, showing the Canada Post building under construction.

Vancouver Archives P106.4, 1956

THE CANADA POST TUNNEL

Pedalling underground, maintenance man Donald MacPherson patrols the Canada Post tunnel, which housed conveyor belt equipment from the main post office to the CPR Station. Vancouver Sun, *Deni Eagland photo, October 20, 1959*

Until 2013, when the building was sold to BC Investment Management Corporation, there was a 2,400-foot (732-metre) tunnel that connected the post office to Waterfront Station. The tunnel, which took five years to dig, ran under Dunsmuir Street to Richards Street, then along Richards and finally zigged left at West Cordova Street. The tunnel was outfitted with two conveyor belts to move the mail and maintained by engineers on bikes. It was used until the mid-1960s, after which mail stopped arriving at the station in bags by train and was instead transported in containers by truck. The machinery was removed, and the tunnel became a favourite location for film shoots (including *Cold Front*, a thriller starring Martin Sheen, and *Friday the 13th Part VIII*) as well as some rocking Halloween parties.

PROJECT 200 AND THE WATERFRONT FREEWAY

Former Vancouver city councillor and urban planner Gordon Price called it the most important thing that never happened to Vancouver—anvd certainly if Project 200, and the rest of the freeway plans, had gone ahead, Vancouver would be virtually unrecognizable today.

The project was approved by Vancouver City Council in December 1968 and the plan was to construct a $340 million freeway system that would connect Vancouver to the Trans-Canada Highway and Highway 99. The freeway would run between Union and Prior Streets; wipe out Strathcona, most of Chinatown and Gastown, part of the West End; plop an ocean parkway along English Bay; and turn Vancouver into a mini Los Angeles.

The Chinatown section of the freeway would connect to a giant ditch along Thurlow Street to a third crossing of Burrard Inlet that would include rapid transit and connect to the North Shore by Stanley Park's Brockton Point, over the world's biggest cable bridge, and then exit at Pemberton Avenue.[18]

As we know now, the only part of this freeway plan that eventuated was the contentious Georgia Viaduct that was built in 1972.

To get a sense of the scope of Project 200, take yourself to the bottom of Granville Street and check out the plaza. Then look up at the thirty-storey tower at 200 Granville Street. Then imagine a forest of office and residential towers, plazas, a large shopping centre including two major department stores, a major hotel and parking for 7,000 cars. The plan would

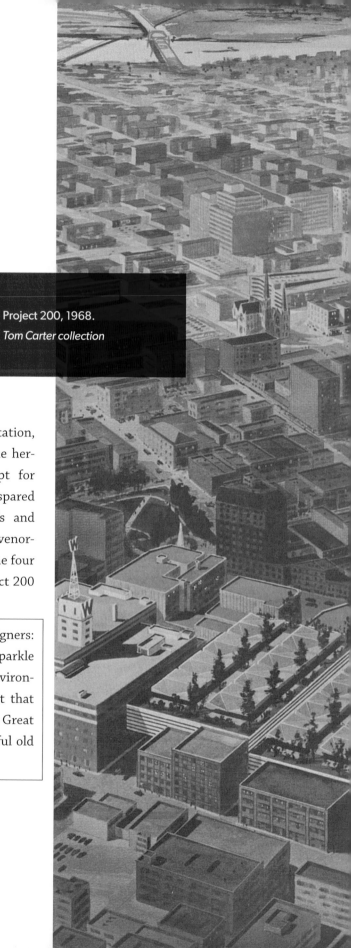

Project 200, 1968.
Tom Carter collection

have knocked out Waterfront Station, the Sinclair Centre and most of the heritage buildings in Gastown except for Woodward's. That building was spared in the plans because Woodward's and Simpson-Sears, along with Grosvenor-Laing and Marathon Realty, were the four major investors that made up Project 200 Properties Limited.

According to the Project 200 designers: "Restaurants and theatres will add sparkle to create a new concept of urban environment." They neglected to point out that Hastings Street was once called the Great White Way, before all those beautiful old sparkling theatres were torn down.

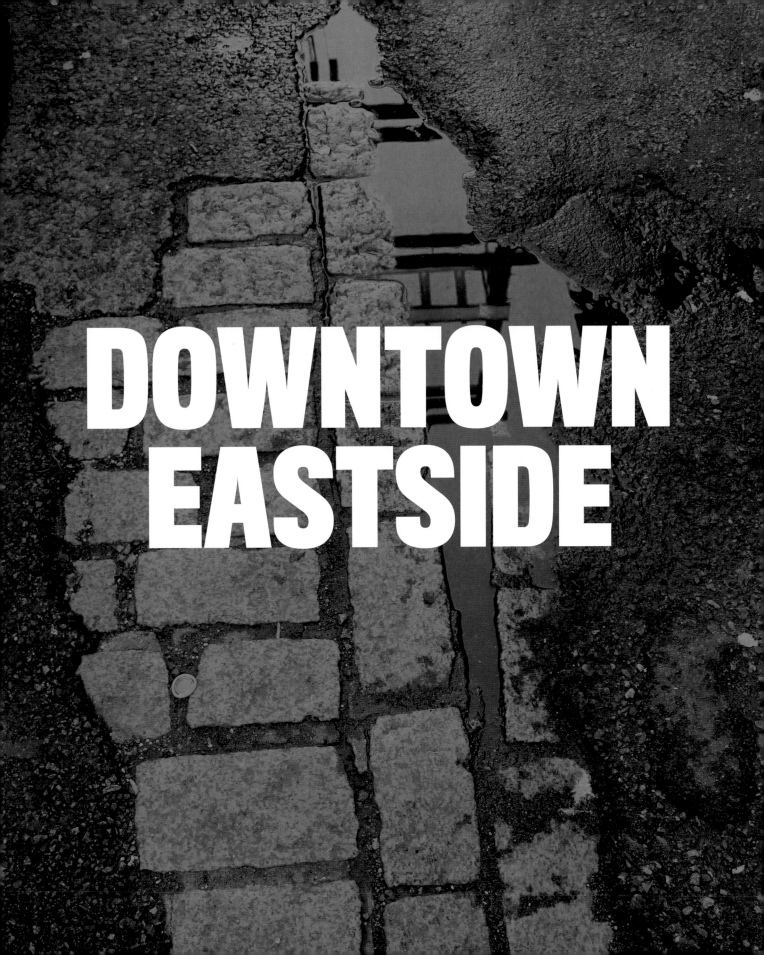

DOWNTOWN EASTSIDE

Hey, what's wrong with this picture? Granville Street looking north from Dunsmuir, ca. 1921.
Vancouver Archives LGN 1026

WE DROVE ON THE LEFT SIDE OF THE ROAD

At six a.m. on Sunday, January 1, 1922, Metro Vancouver and Vancouver Island switched from driving on the left side of the road to driving on the right—and thus became one of the last areas in Canada to change over.[1] The rest of the province had switched on July 15, 1920, but the BC Electric Railway had needed more time to switch over its streetcars, interurbans and tracks. There was a "walk right, drive right" movement and ads in the *Province* and *Vancouver Sun*, while the *World* ran a competition to help citizens escape becoming roadkill. The *Province* predicted there would be "wild confusion at all the great nerve centres of the traffic system," but except for a few drunks from the night before who took the streetcar in the wrong direction, it was as anticlimactic as the Y2K fears of a global computer crash at the turn of the year 2000.

THE HASTINGS GREAT WHITE WAY

In the early twentieth century, the section of Hastings Street that runs through the middle of the Downtown Eastside was known as the Hastings Great White Way after Broadway, New York City's theatre district. And, looking at photos from that time, you can see that it was beautiful. The sidewalks glowed from the light bulbs that ringed the theatre marquees, and all types of theatres and restaurants lined the five blocks from Victory Square to Main Street. In 1913, for instance, Vancouver's theatre district included eight movie theatres, as well as live venues like the Pantages and the Empress. Over the years, the city has managed to destroy all evidence of these theatres.

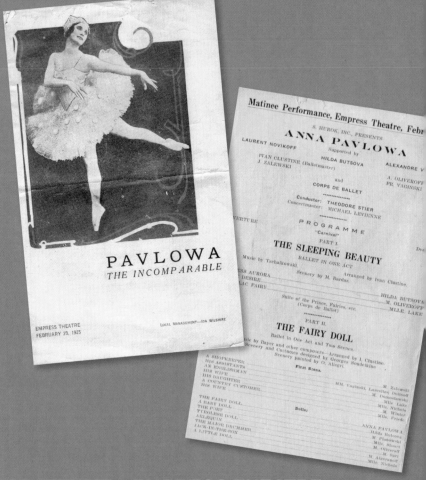

PAVLOWA
THE INCOMPARABLE

EMPRESS THEATRE
FEBRUARY 23, 1925

LOCAL MANAGEMENT—IDA WILSHIRE

EMPRESS THEATRE
(1908–40)

ABOVE LEFT Anna Pavlova at the Empress Theatre, 1925.
Tom Carter collection

ABOVE RIGHT Empress Theatre program, 1925.
Tom Carter collection

LEFT 292 East Hastings, 1909 postcard.
Tom Carter collection

PANTAGES THEATRE
(1907–2011)

152 East Hastings, date unknown.
Neil Whaley collection

PRINCESS (LUX) THEATRE
(1906–2000)

55 East Hastings Street, ca. 1920.
Vancouver Archives 371-867

PANTAGES THEATRE #2
(BEACON, MAJESTIC AND HASTINGS ODEON) (1917–67)

Majestic (Pantages) 20 West Hastings Street, 1964.
Vancouver Archives 447-349

REX THEATRE
(1913–59)

25 West Hastings Street, 1914.
Vancouver Archives 99-240

COLUMBIA/
NATIONAL THEATRE
(1908–'80s)

LEFT Columbia Theatre, 58 West Hastings Street, 1920.
Vancouver Archives 99-3293

BELOW The two theatres were repurposed into Wosk's appliance store: the "House of Quality," 1981.
Vancouver Archives 779-E17.13

SAVING THE PANTAGES THEATRE

In 2008, artist, historian and heritage advocate Tom Carter went for a tour of the Pantages Theatre and listened to Marc Williams of Worthington Properties talk about his plans for the theatre. It was the first time Tom had been inside since going to see a Charlie Chaplin movie with his parents in the 1970s, and he was pleased to see that the beautiful 100-year-old theatre remained salvageable.

Williams had big ideas. He wanted to spend $26 million to restore the theatre and turn it over to the Pantages Theatre Arts Society to manage in time for the 2010 Winter Olympics. The intention was that it would become home to three resident opera and theatre companies. Williams wanted to spend another $30 million to build social housing on the adjacent property, but to do this he needed a heritage density bonus transfer from the city, which would allow him to build more floor space on another building.

It was the kind of deal that happened all over the city. The density bonus transfer program made restoring heritage buildings financially feasible for developers—and it was credited for saving many of Vancouver's heritage buildings. But the city placed a moratorium on density transfers and refused to budge on the Pantages. The restoration plan that Williams had put together fell through, and in September 2008, he offered to sell the theatre to the city instead. By the end of 2009, the city was still dithering, and even Heritage Vancouver, which had identified the Pantages as the city's most important threatened heritage site in 2010, felt the theatre had deteriorated past the point of saving, and they stepped away.

"We were pushing the city to take action, right up to when the bricks were being palleted," says Heritage Vancouver's Patrick Gunn. Shortly after that, a parking meter was thrown through its roof leaving the theatre open to the elements and a burning television set flung from a window in the Regent Hotel started a fire. "The theatre went down even faster—water damage, no heat and structural issues. But it finally hit a point in late 2011 that it was so far gone, nobody was willing to throw any more money into it."

The Pantages Theatre was the oldest remaining vaudeville theatre in Western Canada. It was the last remaining reminder of the once-vibrant theatre district along Hastings Street. Over the years it had been known by a number of names, such as the Royal, State, Queen, Avon, City Nights and Sung Sing.

In the 1930s, it survived a fire in the projectionist's booth, a bomb that had been placed by the ticket office and the Depression. Whereas the fight to save the Pantages took years, it took no time at all for the city to issue a demolition permit.

Tom is furious that there wasn't the will to save the Pantages. But if the actual theatre couldn't be saved, then he at least wanted to salvage some of its parts. People had already stolen some of the ornate pink and gold plaster, thinking that the paint and gilt were real gold.

The theatre was being dismantled by hand in an attempt to save the first-growth timber and bricks (a large archway from the theatre is part of the Urban Fare gourmet grocery store in False Creek). The delay gave Tom time to rescue some of the plasterwork, theatre seats, blueprints, ledger books and promotional materials.

Local historian John Atkin put Tom in touch with the demolition crew. "I said to one of the demo guys, 'What would it take to rescue this?'" says Tom. "And he said, 'Just come with money.'" Each morning, Tom showed up at the site with cash to buy whatever was being torn apart that day. "The prices were really cheap when I first started, and then they got more expensive," he says. "I'd show up and they'd say, 'We want $100,' and I'd say, 'I don't have $100 on me.' And I'd come back

Heritage advocates Jason Vanderhill, Tom Carter and Robert McNutt saving plaster from the Pantages Theatre from demolition.
John Atkin photo

the next day to buy it and they'd say, 'It's under that pile of rubble.' I was buying important stuff from really crazy people."

In 2011, the city retrieved some items from the building before it was demolished. A few pieces went up at the public entrance to the new condos that were built on the site, and the rest were given to the Vancouver Heritage Foundation. A few years later, the VHF sold off the pieces at a garage sale. Tom was told that either he could pay $300 for the plasterwork or it would be taking up space in the landfill. Tom bought the plaster. He picked up more salvaged items from another collector who had bought them from the demolition crew.

Eventually, Tom would like to see the saved pieces of the Pantages restored, conserved, mounted and exhibited next to photos of the old theatre to show where they were situated. It's not the same as having the real thing, but it's better than nothing.

"We could have had this jewel of a theatre with killer acoustics. We could have kept the original streetscape with the Blue Eagle Cafe and the original facades. We could have had housing, shops, offices and the theatre. It could have all been saved, if we'd just had somebody at city hall with a bit of vision and guts."

LEFT Pilaster crest from the Pantages Theatre.
Tom Carter collection

BELOW The last days of the Pantages Theatre, April 2011.
Courtesy Heritage Vancouver

THE REGENT HOTEL

The first time I met Judy Graves was in April 2014. She and John Atkin had planned a tour of some of the oldest buildings in the Downtown Eastside. Judy, with her decades of contacts with city officials, building owners and street people, would get them into the buildings, and John, with his intimate knowledge of the city's architecture and social history, was going to provide perspective. They asked Tom Carter to join them, Tom invited me, and we met at the Ovaltine Cafe on East Hastings for breakfast. We named our little group Exploring Historians (EH!).

We started at the Carnegie Community Centre at Main and Hastings, completed in 1903, and I fell in love with Ken Clarke's sculptures that are on display there. Up until a few years ago, Ken worked out of the Hungry Thumbs Studio at 233 Main Street, and when we visited that day, the

basement still had the original barbershop. Although about seven decades have gone by since it was used for that purpose, the white tiled floors were still intact, the barbershop mirror and remnants of a bathhouse remained.

We toured Orange Hall on Gore and East Hastings, built in 1907, and the Smilin' Buddha Cabaret, a big part of Vancouver's underground music scene from 1952 until the early 1990s. It's now an indoor skate park and restaurant. And then the four of us toured the Regent Hotel, which was then operating as single room occupancy accommodation.

We were standing outside a room on the fifth floor when a rat the size of my miniature schnauzer blew past. I just managed to stop myself from vaulting on top of John's shoulders (the tallest structure in the

Exploring Historians John Atkin, Eve Lazarus, Tom Carter and Judy Graves at the Ovaltine Cafe, April 2014.

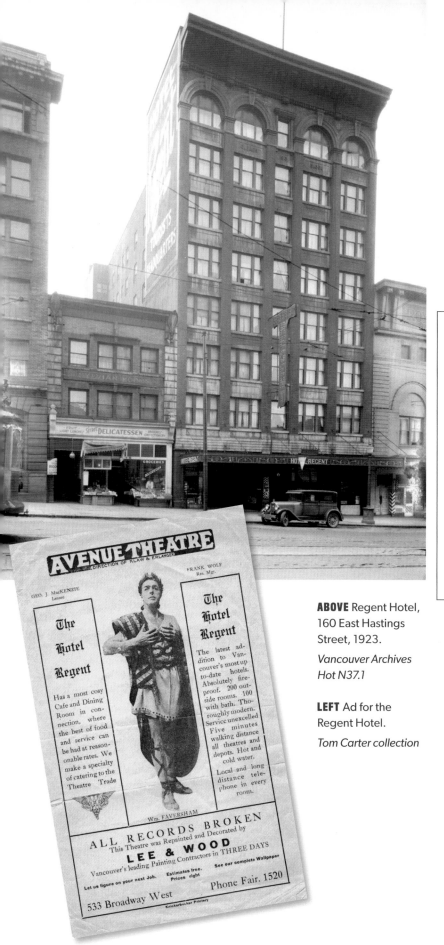

hallway). John, it turns out, doesn't just know buildings and neighbourhoods—he also knows rats. He explained that because rats are nearly blind, they don't run around things (like people) but stick to the wall and let their whiskers help them navigate instead. The Regent Hotel was a step up from living on the street, but only barely—residents fought a daily battle with bedbugs, cockroaches, mice and these giant rats.

The Regent Hotel was a ritzy place when it opened a century ago. Traces of opulence could still be seen in the wood floors and marble staircase, which once swept guests down to the lobby. As the Regent's first brochure boasts, the hotel was five minutes' walking distance from all theatres, a half block from the Carnegie Library and one block from city hall. It had a cafe that offered the "choicest that the management can procure," rooms that were "all light and airy"—about half with private baths—and a telephone in every one.

ABOVE Regent Hotel, 160 East Hastings Street, 1923.

Vancouver Archives Hot N37.1

LEFT Ad for the Regent Hotel.

Tom Carter collection

The city closed the old hotel down in 2018 because of health and safety concerns and in 2020 was still attempting to expropriate the Regent and the Balmoral Hotel, another single room occupancy building across the road, from the slumlords who have owned them both since 1989.

JUDY GRAVES

Judy Graves
outside the Carnegie
Community Centre at
Main and Hastings.
*Eve Lazarus photo,
April 2014*

Before Judy Graves retired in 2013, she had spent thirty-three years employed by the City of Vancouver, representing the marginalized and homeless residents of the Downtown Eastside. The following year she received a phone call from Mayor Gregor Robertson. He told Judy he had great news—she was being awarded the highest honour the City of Vancouver had to give: the Freedom of the City Award for her work in building a better community. She wouldn't be the only recipient. Jimmy Pattison, CEO of the Jim Pattison Group, would also receive the award at a ceremony at the Vancouver Playhouse.

While Judy lives in the West End and has spent three decades walking city blocks to find and help people, Pattison is one of the wealthiest individuals in Canada. His companies employ more than 35,000 people and he has been presented with both the Order of BC and the Order of Canada. He has donated millions to health care institutions.

The Freedom of the City Award comes with a lifetime of free parking at city meters—a strange gift for a green city to be awarding. Pattison clearly doesn't need free parking, and Judy, well, Judy doesn't drive. Never has. In Mayor Robertson's initial phone call to her he asked for Judy's driver's licence number and car licence plate.

"I said, 'how about a bus pass?'" says Judy. "That was the end of the conversation. Someone from his office got back to me and said, 'we can't do that.'"

No reason given.

So, Judy mostly walks to where she needs to go. If she needs a bus, she pays for it herself, as she always has.

VICTORY SQUARE: WHAT WAS THERE BEFORE?

Before Victory Square was home to the cenotaph, Vancouver's memorial to citizens who lost their lives in the First World War, it was a happening part of the city known as Government Square, because it was the site of the first provincial courthouse. The impressive domed building was operational by 1890 and was the first major building constructed in the city outside of Gastown. It soon became apparent that it was too small for the growing city, and within a few years it was given a large addition with a grand staircase and portico facing Hastings Street. Other buildings started to spring up around the courthouse. In 1898, Thomas Flack, who had made his fortune in the Klondike Gold Rush, wanted to see an impressive building bear his name. The Flack Block is still there, at the corner of Hastings and Cambie Streets.

The original courthouse lasted just twenty years. It was demolished when the new law courts opened on West Georgia Street in 1912.

The square, which is actually a triangle, is bounded by Hastings, Cambie, Pender and Hamilton Streets. It didn't remain empty for long. By 1914, it was filled with a large tent, which was used by military recruiters to sign up soldiers to fight in the First World War. Then, in 1917, up went the Evangelistic Tabernacle, but the church too was short lived. The land became Victory Square in 1922, and two years later enough public money had been raised to build the cenotaph. The inscription, facing Hastings Street, reads: "Their name liveth for evermore: in memory of those who gave their lives in the service of our country (1914–1918)."

1 Vancouver's original courthouse, ca. 1893.
   Vancouver Archives Bu N13

2 The Evangelistic Tabernacle under
   construction, 1917.
   Vancouver Archives Bu P173

3 Victory Square, ca. 1925.
   Vancouver Archives 99-3054

4 Victory Square in 2020.
   Eve Lazarus photo

THE DOMINION BUILDING

There's a story that keeps popping up, usually around Halloween, that drives me crazy. There are several different versions, but essentially, it goes like this: architect John Shaw Helyer designed the Dominion Building, and then on opening day in 1910, he threw himself down the spiral staircase to his death. Great story, but Helyer died in 1919 after never fully recovering from a stroke. But just because that's an urban myth, it doesn't mean the building can't have its own great story.

This overdressed red-brick and yellow terracotta structure, with its oddly shaped beaux arts roof, comes from a time when architectural sculpture helped shape Vancouver. The tower looks like a nineteenth-century Parisian building stretched up into a skyscraper. It's this eccentricity that I love about the building—that and the way it dominates that intersection of Hastings and Cambie.

It's a reminder that this part of the city was once the heart of Vancouver, with the Woodward's Building to the east, two of the daily newspapers and department stores within walking distance and the original law courts across the road, where Victory Square now sits.

The Dominion Building was financed in part by the flamboyant entrepreneur Alvo von Alvensleben. In the ten years he lived in Vancouver, he brought millions of dollars of German investment to the city, and bought up large tracts of real estate. Among his holdings were a hunting lodge in North Vancouver and houses in Pitt Meadows, Surrey and Washington State, the latter two still known as Alien Acres and Spy House. He lived at what is now Crofton House, a girls' school in Kerrisdale, and he developed the Wigwam Inn at Indian Arm into a luxury resort.

Before going fabulously broke in 1914, Alvensleben had amassed a personal fortune, with business interests that included mining, forestry and fishing. That year, the Dominion Trust Company collapsed, and Alvensleben was reviled as a suspected German spy in the climate of fear surrounding the First World War. When war broke out he was sailing from Germany to the United States and on arrival was greeted with the news that the Canadian government had confiscated all his holdings and he would be arrested if he set foot in Canada. His Canadian-born wife, Edith, and their three children grabbed all the cash and jewellery on hand and joined Alvensleben in Seattle.

At the time of writing, Jacqui Cohen, CEO of the now defunct Army & Navy department stores, owned the building and rented it to the same eclectic bunch that have always been attracted to its look and feel. Writers, barristers, accountants, artists, unionists and film directors rub shoulders in the elevators, which display archival photos dating back to the building's birth.

Dominion Building, 1969.

Vancouver Archives 1135-13

ON TOP OF THE WORLD

In 2013, I ticked off one of the items on my bucket list: to see Vancouver from inside the cupola on top of the Sun Tower. It took a ride in the elevator to the seventeenth floor, a climb up a couple of flights of stairs into the dome, and then a scramble up a steep ladder. Even with all the skyscrapers that have popped up to overshadow it, the view from the cupola of this 1912 building is breathtaking.

The building itself is a piece of art. Details include a marble staircase, brass key plates on the office doors, and nine topless maidens sculpted by Charles Marega that flank the eighth floor. L.D. Taylor was part of a consortium that built the tower, originally named the World Building, after his newspaper, the *Vancouver Daily World*. Taylor still holds the record as the longest-serving mayor of Vancouver. He was first elected to the office in 1910, and served off and on until 1934 for a total of eleven years. Taylor couldn't withstand the real estate crash of 1913. By 1915 he was in dire financial straits and sold his share of the building and was forced to sell his newspaper to pay off creditors.

The Sun Tower from Pender Street and Main, ca. 1986.

Dietmar Waber photo, Neil Whaley collection

ABOVE *Vancouver Sun* photographer and reporter on the roof of the Sun Tower, January 1946.
VPL Special Collections #26911

RIGHT A crowd watches Harry Gardiner (the "Human Fly") scale the World Building in 1918.
Vancouver Archives 1376-113

Bekins, a Seattle-based moving company, owned the building from 1924 until it sold it to the *Vancouver Sun* publishers in 1937, after a fire destroyed their building right across the street. The *Sun* occupied the building until 1965, when the paper joined with the *Province* to become Pacific Press and moved to Granville and Sixth Avenue. The Press Club, of course, moved with them.

One of the biggest misconceptions about the Sun Tower is that it has a copper roof that has turned green from oxidation. In reality, the original copper cladding was replaced long ago. Now it's just terracotta tile painted green.

VANCOUVER'S FIRST HOSPITAL

Where other cities value heritage buildings, public space and art, Vancouver, it seems, has a thing for parking lots.

Since 1970, a cavernous concrete EasyPark lot that faces West Pender Street has taken up the city block from Cambie Street to Beatty Street, but long before that, it was the site of Vancouver's first hospital. The buildings included a men's surgical ward, a maternity ward, a tuberculosis ward and the city morgue, which faced Beatty Street. The hospital was built in 1888, and photos show a compound of brick buildings with wooden balconies set back from the street, flower gardens and a picket fence.

By the turn of the twentieth century, the fifty-bed hospital was too small for Vancouver's growing population, so a new hospital was built in Fairview in 1906 and became the Vancouver General Hospital we know now. Our first city hospital was repurposed into the headquarters for McGill University College of BC until 1911, and Social Services (the City Relief and Employment Department) took up offices there until the late 1940s. By 1950, all the hospital buildings were gone. Now all that's left is a heritage plaque affixed to the parking garage.

Vancouver Hospital,
530 Cambie Street,
1902.
Vancouver Archives
Bu P369

A BRIEF HISTORY OF VANCOUVER'S CITY HALLS

Before we had city hall on West Twelfth Avenue in Mount Pleasant, it was housed in a number of interesting buildings. One of the earliest photos shows a city council meeting in a tent shortly after the Great Fire wiped out most of the city in 1886. That year, the Sentell brothers were contracted to build the first city hall at 149–151 Powell Street—a two-storey wooden structure. It took only a month to build and its budget came in under $1,300. But the city couldn't afford the tab, so the Sentell brothers locked them out until they came up with the cash.

The building quickly became too small for the growing city, and when David Oppenheimer was elected mayor in 1888, city hall moved into his grocery warehouse at Powell and Columbia. The building is now rehabilitated and owned by rock star Bryan Adams.

Frederick Cope replaced Oppenheimer as mayor in 1892, and in 1898 city hall moved to Market Hall on Main Street (Westminster Avenue until 1910), just south of the Carnegie Library, where it remained for the next three decades.

In 1929, city hall moved to the Holden Block at 16 East Hastings Street, which was designed in 1911 by William T. Whiteway—the same architect who designed the Sun Tower and Kathryn Maynard's swanky Alexander Street brothel.

The potential sites for our current city hall included: a new building at Main and Hastings; Thornton Park at Main and Terminal Streets; Burrard and Davie Streets as proposed by Harland Bartholomew's 1928 plan for the city of Vancouver; and the current site at Twelfth and Cambie. Mayor Gerry McGeer lobbied hard for an Art Deco city hall building at the Mount Pleasant site. It was the first time a major Canadian city built its city hall outside the city centre, when construction began in 1936.

1   149–151 Powell Street, ca. 1893.
    Vancouver Archives City P54

2   Oppenheimer Warehouse, 1898.
    Vancouver Archives Bu P683

3   Market Hall, 1928.
    Vancouver Archives City N12

4   Vancouver City Hall, 1936.
    Vancouver Archives 677-117

FROM CITY HALL TO BRYAN ADAMS'S RECORDING STUDIO

Vancouver rock legend Bryan Adams has collected a ton of hardware over the years, but the one I find the most interesting is the Heritage Award he received in 1998 for transforming a derelict Gastown warehouse into a world-class recording studio.

When Adams bought the brick building at the corner of Powell and Columbia Streets in 1991, it was abandoned and abused. The restoration took seven years and cost $5 million, including the purchase price. The three-storey building has large windows to let in lots of natural light, a massive main studio on the second floor and a mixing suite on the third floor.

The Victorian-style warehouse is the oldest brick building in the city. Built by David Oppenheimer, a German immigrant and Vancouver's second mayor (1888–91) for his wholesale grocery and provisions business. Today, it hosts bands and rock stars including AC/DC, Elton John, Bon Jovi, the Tragically Hip, Metallica and Michael Bublé.

100 Powell Street,
2014.

Eve Lazarus photo

RECOGNIZING BLACK HISTORY: THE CANADA POST STAMPS

Nora Hendrix and Fielding William Spotts featured on the 2014 Canada Post stamp commemorating Black History Month.

Courtesy Canada Post

In February 2014, Canada Post came out with two stamps in recognition of Black History Month. One shows Hogan's Alley, the unofficial name for an area near Union and Main Streets and home to much of Vancouver's early Black community. The other is of Nora Hendrix and Fielding William Spotts. The photo of Spotts was taken in 1935, and it shows the seventy-five-year-old standing outside his home at 217½ Prior Street in Hogan's Alley, which would be bulldozed out of existence four decades later to make way for the Georgia Viaduct. On the stamp, Spotts stands next to a youthful Nora Hendrix, who lived to be 100, spent much of her life in Strathcona and became famous for her grandson, rocker Jimi Hendrix. According to the city directory of 1930, Spotts ran a shoeshine business at 724 Main Street.

I was curious how Canada Post chose these images, so I called Eugene Knapik, then the Toronto-based media relations manager. Turns out it's quite a process. A committee of twelve selects the subject matter. In 2014, our one representative from Vancouver was artist Ken Lum. He joined a panel of designers, philatelists (stamp collectors), curators and, curiously, Toronto economist David Foot, who wrote *Boom, Bust & Echo*.

I also wondered who buys stamps these days. Turns out that although few of us mail letters, there's still a large worldwide demand for stamps. Canada Post churns out about sixty different stamps every year. Eugene said anyone is welcome to suggest a stamp—it takes about two years from inception to find its way to an envelope.

THE MISSING CANADIAN NATIONAL STEAMSHIP TERMINAL

Before CRAB Park was created in 1987, there was a funky Spanish colonial–style building that sat on the pier at the foot of Main Street. Built in 1931 as the terminal for the Canadian National Steamship Company, the terminal was accessed by a roadway over the Canadian Pacific Railway tracks.

While the CPR owned the Princess line of steamboats, the competition—Canadian National—had a healthy line of Princes—Henry, David, Robert, Charles, William and George—until the Second World War, when steamship service dropped, and then stopped altogether in the 1950s.

By 1973, the terminal was in full swing as the Oompapa Restaurant, and later the Happy Bavarian Inn. Over the next decade, it became the Dock and then O'Hara's, before being demolished in 1983.

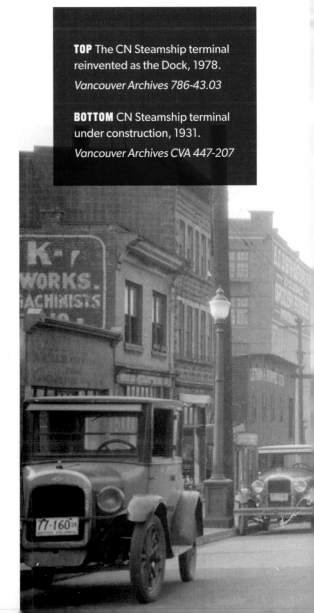

TOP The CN Steamship terminal reinvented as the Dock, 1978.
Vancouver Archives 786-43.03

BOTTOM CN Steamship terminal under construction, 1931.
Vancouver Archives CVA 447-207

ART, HISTORY AND A MISSION

In 2016, I was a board member for the Vancouver Historical Society when the Vancouver Fraser Port Authority contacted us and asked what we'd like to do with a nearly nine-foot- (three-metre-) high sculpture made from BC granite that had been sitting on their land at the foot of Dunlevy Avenue since a previous board had commissioned it fifty years before.

Since this was the first any of us had heard of it, we did some research and found that, in 1966, the VHS had contributed funds toward a $4,500 three-piece sculpture created by Gerhard Class to mark the 100th anniversary of Hastings Mill, the first industrial operation in what eventually became Vancouver.

We took a field trip to check it out. It's a beautiful piece of art consisting of three free-standing forms, each a different height.

The problem for the port was that the sculpture sat in a garden behind the Mission to Seafarers: Flying Angels Club. The port owns the land on which the house stands and leases it back to the mission for one dollar a year. Over the decades, the garden shrank as the port expanded. In the long term, the fate of the house is threatened, which is tragic because the building and its location are an essential part of Vancouver's history.

BC Mills Timber and Trading Company built what is now the Mission to Seafarers house in 1906 as the sawmill's offices. The building was a showplace for the company's prefabricated houses, schools, banks and churches. The walls of each office were panelled in a different type of wood—fir, hemlock, red cedar and balsam—which were painted over after the mill closed in 1928 and the Vancouver Harbour Commissioners moved in. The National Harbours Board owned the house next, and the Mission to Seafarers took possession in the early 1970s where they would provide assistance and care to seaman from more than ninety countries.

For centuries before, the Coast Salish people knew the land that is now part of Strathcona as Kumkumalay ("big leaf maple trees"). In 1865, it became the site of the Hastings Mill, the mill store (which moved to Kitsilano in 1930) and Vancouver's first public school. The unemployed set up camp

The Hastings Mill sculpture in its new home, 2018.

Carol Macfarlane photo, Vancouver Fraser Port Authority

cul-de-sac. To get there you have to take the Main Street overpass, and then go along East Waterfront Road.

At the time the VHS became involved, the port was planning to install shore power transformers in the garden where the sculpture sat. The Port Authority's Carol Macfarlane went to enormous lengths to find a new home for the sculpture. "It reminded me of an iceberg," says Carol. "The monument is eight and a half feet [two and a half metres] tall, but the underground is over three feet [one metre] deep and seven feet [two metres] wide."

When the VHS realized the sheer lunacy of having to work with three levels of government to make the sculpture more accessible somewhere else, we opted simply to move it to the front of the house.

Gerhard Class was a well-known sculptor who came to Canada from Germany in 1951, taught at the Vancouver School of Art and worked mainly in stone and steel. He died in 1997, but I was able to track down his daughter, Dr Sabrina Class, who put Carol in touch with Paul Slipper, a student of her father's. Paul cleaned the sculpture, sealed up the rough areas, waxed the smooth surfaces of the granite and replaced a piece of plywood in the centre with a new carved slab of granite for stability. He then supervised the move and, in a nice addition, installed wood chips at the base to represent the old mill.

here during the worst of the Depression. Hastings Mill was a significant employer of Japanese Canadians, which led to the creation of Japantown situated along nearby Powell Street.

Once easily accessible and surrounded by gardens that led to the waterfront, the mission's heritage building is now wrapped in a chain-link of security that has marooned the house in a kind of

$1.49 DAY
AT WOODWARD'S

CKNW radio station creative director Tony Antonias wrote a catchy jingle in 1958, and even though Woodward's department store closed its doors in 1993, it's still familiar to most British Columbians who are over the age of thirty-five.

A long-time New Westminster resident, and fellow Aussie, Tony started as a copywriter at the station in 1955. He stayed there for the next forty years—to the day. Tony died in January 2019, but he talked to me about the jingle, and his career at CKNW, in 2018—on the jingle's sixtieth anniversary. He told me that the tune came about almost by accident, after he hit the key on a new typewriter and it made a loud ding—$1.49 Day. When he hit the key again, it made another ding— yup, $1.49 Day. Tuesday.

Tony wrote the jingle on February 17, 1958, recorded it over the Easter weekend and then Woodward's took six weeks to decide to use it. "Everybody wants to know how the $1.49 jingle came to be," he told me. "I've scripted it and I've got it on CDs and they love hearing it."

Charles Woodward opened his store at the corner of West Hastings and Abbott Streets in 1903, turning Hastings Street into a main shopping and business centre. The store was a retailing force until its bankruptcy ninety years later. Charles's son Percival Archibald Woodward ran the Woodward's department stores for many years. Known as Mr P.A. to his employees, and Puggy to his friends, he created Woodward's famous food floor—and with it, turned the entire concept of retailing on its head. Forestry magnate and philanthropist H.R. MacMillan once called him the best businessman raised on the Pacific Coast, yet he never finished high school.

It was Puggy's idea in 1927 to build a seventy-five-foot- (twenty-three-metre-) high beacon to act as a giant billboard for the store. The tower held a searchlight that threw out a two-million-candlepower beam that revolved six times a minute and could be seen from Vancouver Island. When the Second World War hit, Puggy was told to turn off the beacon because it was such a big target, and in the late 1950s, the big *W* took its place. Puggy predicted that malls were the wave of the future and was himself a driving force behind the Park Royal Shopping Centre, which, in 1950, was the first shopping mall in Canada. He was also a philanthropist with an interest in medical research and left his vast estate to the Mr. and Mrs. P.A. Woodward's Foundation when he died in 1968—ten years after Tony created the iconic Woodward's jingle.

Christmas shoppers for $1.49 Day at Woodward's department store in Vancouver.
Province, *Doug Todd photo*

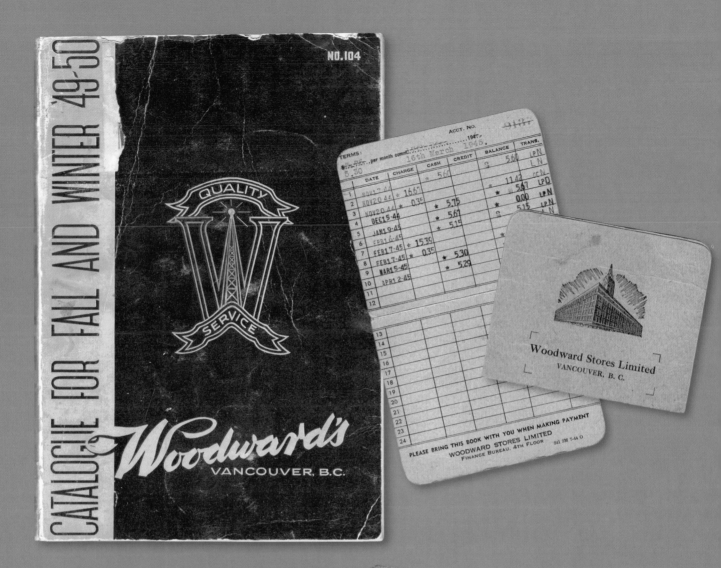

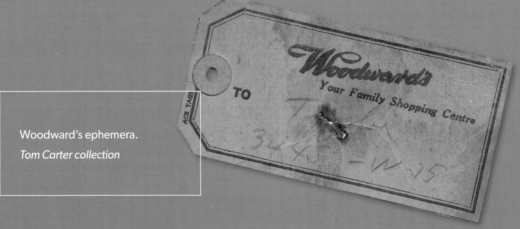

Woodward's ephemera.
Tom Carter collection

THE MISSING ELEVATOR OPERATORS OF VANCOUVER

Angus McIntyre started as a bus driver for BC Hydro in 1969 and remembers $1.49 Day at Woodward's store well: "Loads were heavier, and we had to make sure to have extra tokens and change ready," he says. "On $1.49 Day, the store was just a solid mass of shoppers."

Angus also spent quite a bit of time inside the store when he wasn't on shift and got to know the elevator operators. One of them occasionally rode his bus home. "The manual elevators were in the centre of the store, and the senior operator was the starter. The starter stood at an information booth on the main concourse near the lifts, and she had a set of castanets. When she saw that a car was full, she would signal the operator with a 'clack-clack,' the gate would slide across and the doors would close. The sound could be heard above the busiest crowds on

$1.49 Day. This was a physical job, since Woodward's elevators had to be levelled at each floor manually, and the interior gate and exterior doors opened by hand as well. Since there were windows in the doors, you could see all the people inside as the car ascended."

Jeanne Nielsen's aunt Vi was an elevator operator at the downtown Eaton's store in the late 1950s and early '60s. "She wore a uniform that had a nice pleated kilt, and I thought she looked very glamorous," says Jeanne.

The Marine Building had eight of the sharpest-looking elevator operators in town. A 1952 classified ad in the *Vancouver Sun* asked for an "elevator operator for permanent position with no Sunday, holiday or evening work. Must be single, neat, well-mannered and between the ages of 18 and 25. Excellent wages. Apply Marine

Building."[2] Three years later, a reporter interviewed an unnamed manager about their "beautiful" operators. "We don't go in for that Hollywood stuff, such as sending the operators to the hairdresser once a week on company expense—a thing that is done by some American companies," a presumably male manager said. "All we ask is that the operators be of neat appearance and of good family and that they stick to the job. We're not looking for girls who regard their job here merely as a stepping stone toward modelling or acting glamour."[3]

Nancy Kern worked as an elevator operator at the Hudson's Bay department store during the summer of 1968. "It was a glamorous job back then," she says. "We had very cool white dresses with stripes and wore white gloves. They paid for us to have our hair done at the Bay beauty salon every week. I even had [US actor and singer] Ed Ames as one of my passengers that summer. I often tell my kids and grandkids that it was probably the most unique job I ever had."

In the early 1970s, there were at least forty buildings in the city that still had operators, including Vancouver City Hall, the Hotel Vancouver, the Sun Tower and all the department stores. "Most large American cities had already automated their lifts, but Vancouver didn't start in earnest until later," Angus tells me.

Angus McIntyre at Kootenay Loop with the Brill trolley bus he drove on city tours on the 125th anniversary of Vancouver's transit system.

Courtesy Angus McIntyre, 2015

"The operator of the elevator in the Hotel Vancouver would, at times, take off quickly, on the long ride to the roof. The feeling in the pit of your stomach was a bit like taking off in the jets of the day," says blog commenter Terry Friesen.

Judy Truelove was a Hotel Vancouver elevator operator in the summer of 1972. "Our uniforms were an ugly olive green, and we wore white gloves," she says. "One of the guys had long hair, so he had to wear a wig. It was a repressive atmosphere, as we were discouraged from interacting with guests or each other. Memorable guests were [tennis star] Arthur Ashe, [BC politician] 'Flying' Phil Gaglardi and delegates to a convention for [the religious group called] the Eckankar."

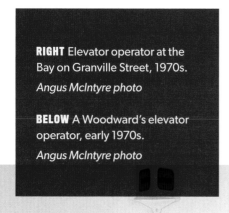

Angus says that the old BC Electric Railway terminal on Carrall Street had elevators that ran on 600 volts direct current, sourced from the trolley bus system. "About a dozen downtown buildings were wired into the trolley system, so if there were a trolley power failure, people would be stuck in the elevators," he says. "The last building to use such power was the Sylvia Hotel. It converted in the 1980s."

The last building to use elevator operators in Vancouver was the Medical Arts Building on Granville Street in 1993. Customers of the Royal Bank on Hastings Street can still ride in a hand-operated elevator to their safety deposit boxes.

THE WOODWARD'S CHRISTMAS WINDOWS

If you ask locals what they remember about Woodward's department store, they'll probably tell you about $1.49 Day and their annual trip to see the store's famous Christmas window displays.

When David Rowland heard that Woodward's was closing in 1993, he phoned up the manager and put in an offer for the store's historic Christmas displays. They agreed on a price, and David became the proud owner of six semi-trailer loads of teddy bears, elves, geese, children, a horse and cart and various storefronts.

In the late 1960s, fourteen-year-old David rode the bus into Vancouver from Cloverdale carrying three samples of puppets and marionettes that he had made. He walked up and down what was then Robsonstrasse trying to interest toy-store owners in buying his merchandise. "They said, 'they are nice little toys, and you are a nice little boy, but come back when you have sold them somewhere else,'" says David. "I was about to give up and I thought, 'Well there's always the Bay.'"

David found the manager of the Bay's Toyland and put his marionettes through their paces. "A lot of people gathered and shoppers started picking up the boxes looking for prices," he says. The manager ordered fifty and had David come in and demonstrate them every Saturday. Later, he invented a coin-operated puppet theatre where you could put in a quarter and lights would turn on and music would play as puppets danced across the stage. He sold three dozen of them to shopping centres around BC. As requests came in to build Santa's castles and other seasonal structures, David's business took off.

Woodward's started getting serious about their Christmas window displays in the 1960s and sent buyers off to New York to bring back different figures. David was hired in the 1970s to create mechanical figures for Toyland and display work for their windows.

When David unpacked his newly acquired Christmas displays in the 1990s, he found at least a dozen different scenes. He looked around for a venue big enough to display them and found himself at Canada Place in downtown Vancouver. Rowland wanted to rent the pieces out, but Canada Place offered to buy them outright. "That wasn't my initial plan, but at the time I had a banker from hell and I needed some capital and so I sold a lot of it to them," he says. David couldn't bear to part with all of them, though, and every other year he sets up a few scenes in buildings around Vancouver.

ABOVE David Rowland with some of the Woodward's figures that he built, 1980s.
Courtesy David Rowland

LEFT Every year, since 2013, Christ Church Cathedral has displayed the former Woodward's nativity scene.
Eve Lazarus photo, 2018

THE TRAIN THAT CROSSED HASTINGS STREET

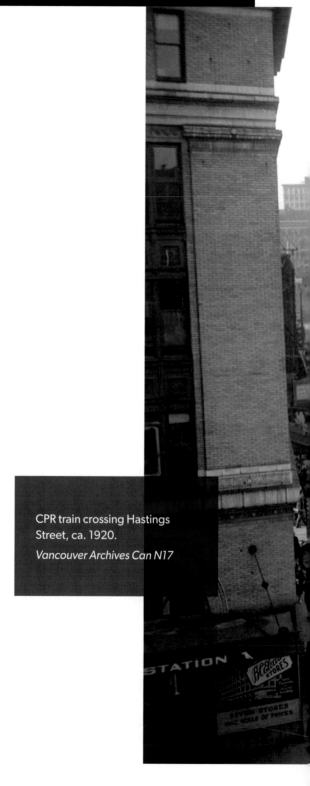

Did you know that a steam train used to run right through downtown Vancouver? I first saw it in one of Tom Carter's paintings: a massive thing chugging across Hastings Street. I stumbled across the train again when I was writing *Blood, Sweat, and Fear: The Story of Inspector Vance, Vancouver's First Forensic Investigator.* I was trying to retrace Inspector John F.C.B. Vance's route from his home in Yaletown by streetcar to his lab at Hastings and Main Street for his first day of work. The 1907 map that I downloaded from Vancouver Archives showed that four large blocks, from Hastings to Water Street and from Cambie to Carrall Street, were occupied by the BC Electric Railway.

The streetcars were already in place by then, in fact they had been since 1891, but the interurban train came later, in 1911 after the BCER opened its terminal at Carrall and West Hastings. That year, more than three miles (five kilometres) of track ran through city streets, originating at the BCER's terminus, and interurban lines ran to New Westminster and Chilliwack. One track off Hastings Street split in two at the terminal, while another track was mostly used for freight and ran between the terminal and the Canadian Pacific Railway line.

At its peak, BCER operated 457 streetcars and 84 interurban lines.[4] The streetcars operated on hydroelectric power generated by BCER subsidiary Vancouver Power Company at Buntzen Lake near Anmore, BC. The BCER's interurban terminal is still there on the corner of Carrall and West Hastings Street. The entrance for the trains is now a window that takes up most of the side of the building.

> If I were putting together a list of the top ten worst decisions when it comes to destroying Vancouver's history and heritage, the switch "from rails to rubber" in the mid-1950s would be right up there with the demolition of the Birks Building and the second Hotel Vancouver.

BC Electric Railway head office at Carrall and West Hastings, ca. 1912.

Vancouver Archives LGN 1159

Essentially, the BCER's decision to move from rails to rubber marked the end of the city's use of streetcars and the interurban system and the introduction of buses. The car was now king, streetcar ridership was dropping and there was no need to spend the money to upgrade and maintain an aging transit system. The last streetcar made its final Vancouver run in 1955. Three years later, the last of the interurbans finished up service in Steveston.

Evidence that we had a streetcar and efficient interurban system hasn't completely disappeared though. The interurban system was made up of five major lines, three that are similar to today's SkyTrain routes: the Expo Line (Central Park Line), the Millennium Line (Burnaby Lake Line) and the Canada Line (Lulu Island Line). The Westminster-Eburne Line connected Marpole to New Westminster, and the Chilliwack Line connected New West to Chilliwack.

BILLY STARK, THE FIRST GAS-POWERED CAR AND CANADA'S FIRST GAS STATION

Billy Stark at the controls of a Curtiss exhibition-type pusher biplane at Minoru Park, April 13, 1912.

Vancouver Archives 371-2333

William "Billy" Stark drove Vancouver's first gas-powered car in 1901. A story in the *Province* described it as a "wheezing one-lung Oldsmobile with a lever for a steering wheel and a bell for a horn."[5] This was when British Columbians still drove on the left side of the road, and Stark was often fined for exceeding the speed limit of ten miles (sixteen kilometres) an hour. He and Bill Annand went into business and opened the first garage and car dealership in the city at 108 East Hastings Street in an old livery stable under the name Vancouver Automobile and Cycle. They moved to Seymour Street in 1907, sold Oldsmobiles and Massey-Harris bicycles, and serviced cars, bikes and boats. The following year, they sold the business to Frank and Fred Begg—who renamed the company Begg Brothers—because Stark decided "there was no future in the automobile business—just a rich man's toy."[6]

Canada's first gas station opened at Cambie and Smithe Streets in 1907. That year, there were 2,131 cars registered in the entire country, so it wasn't surprising that a busy day at the pumps meant three cars fuelling up. By the outbreak of the First World War, there were 50,000 cars in the country, and by 1930, there were just under 100,000 cars registered in BC alone.[7]

Billy Stark may have left the car business prematurely, but his need for speed turned him onto airplanes, and he was BC's first aviator. By April 1912, he had made more than 200 flights, and on April 13, he took his seventy-five-horsepower biplane, capable of travelling seventy miles (110 kilometres) an hour, for a flight at Minoru Park on Lulu Island.

Canada's first gas station at Cambie and Smithe, ca. 1911.
Vancouver Archives 389-2

LARWILL PARK AND THE BUS DEPOT

TOP The circus comes to the Cambie Street Grounds, May 1926.

Vancouver Archives 99-1550

BOTTOM Inside the bus depot at Larwill Park, 1979.

Angus McIntyre photo

Larwill Park was originally known as the Cambie Street Grounds, a park with sports fields, and, being opposite the Beatty Street Drill Hall, it operated at times as a military drill ground. The park was named after Al Larwill, who, the story goes, was made caretaker after squatting in a shack on the land for many years. He was given a house on a corner where he stored sports equipment and allowed team members to use his dining room to change.

In 1946, the city leased the land to BC Electric for a bus yard, and Charles Bentall of the Dominion Construction Company built the bus depot. Pacific Stage Lines, Greyhound Lines, Squamish Coach Lines and others operated out of the terminal until car culture struck in the 1950s and '60s and some of the companies went under.

In 1993, the bus depot moved to Pacific Central Station on Station Street, and Larwill Park became a huge parking lot bounded by Cambie, Dunsmuir, Beatty and Georgia Streets. The plan is for the city to turn the site over to the Vancouver Art Gallery.

DUNSMUIR TUNNEL

While you're stuck for an hour on the Lions Gate Bridge or crawling over the Ironworkers Memorial Bridge, it may be comforting to know that traffic problems, just like the price of real estate, have always been an issue in Vancouver.

As early as 1914, there were calls for an end to the Carrall and Hastings Street crossing, where freight and passenger trains could hold up traffic for up to an hour a day getting from the CPR yards on Burrard Inlet to the yards at False Creek.

The train crossing was still there a decade later when a frustrated *Vancouver Daily World* reporter named F.W. Luce wrote, "Lifelong friendships have been formed while waiting for a CPR train to thump its leisurely way along the Carrall Street level crossing. Complete strangers will scrape acquaintance by making a bet on how long they will have to wait. Half an hour later they will still be sitting on the sidewalk."[8]

The crossing was still there in 1929 when a *Vancouver Sun* editorial called it an obstacle to the growth of Vancouver. "It costs Vancouver people thousands of dollars. It depreciates real estate values in the neighborhood to the extent of hundreds of thousands of dollars."[9]

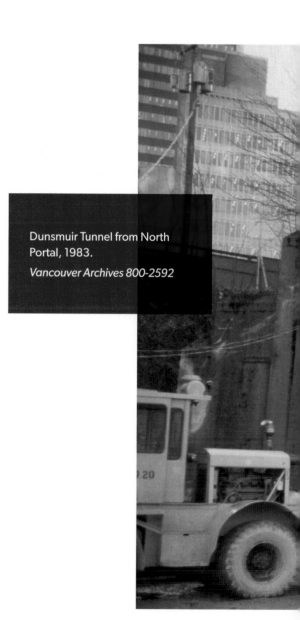

Dunsmuir Tunnel from North Portal, 1983.
Vancouver Archives 800-2592

The Dunsmuir Tunnel opened in July 1932 and was 4,600 feet (1,400 metres) long and lined throughout with concrete. Steam engines now followed a 190-degree arc from Waterfront Station, passing under Thurlow, crossing to Burrard and then going under Dunsmuir to Cambie, where the tunnel cut under the old bus depot at Larwill Park and came out by the Georgia Viaduct.

Andy Cassidy worked for CPR at the Drake Street roundhouse until it closed in 1981.

"I travelled through that tunnel daily for years, either on the passenger cars going from the station to the coach yard or, later on, while taking the locomotives from the shop over to the waiting train at the station," he says. "I used to have to adjust the locomotive headlights regularly on the way through."

The last train went through the tunnel in August 1982. The tunnel then underwent a $10 million renovation and was repurposed as SkyTrain's Expo Line, with the westbound track now stacked above the eastbound track. The new tunnel, with the Burrard and Granville Street stations built inside, opened in time for Expo 86. The eastern entrance to the tunnel was a concrete Art Deco portal set into the base of the cliff below Beatty Street. It was demolished to make way for the Cosmo, a twenty-seven-storey tower that opened in 2012. The western end of the tunnel is under Portal Park at West Hastings and Thurlow Streets—a City of Vancouver park built on a concrete roof in June 1986.

TOP CPR steam engine #3716 leaving the Dunsmuir Tunnel, May 1980.

Courtesy Jacqueline Allan, Allan's Digital Media Memories

BOTTOM An MLW S-3 yard engine pulling a passenger train through the Dunsmuir Tunnel, 1959.

Andy Cassidy collection

SKWACHÀYS
LODGE

31 West Pender Street as the Wingate Hotel, 1977.

Vancouver Archives 1135-19

I first heard of the Skwachàys Lodge in 2015, when it appeared on *The Guardian*'s top ten list of hotels in Vancouver that "celebrate art, history and the best in food and drink." It was promoted to *The Guardian*'s British readership as "Vancouver's newest boutique hotel in the city's gentrifying downtown eastside."[10]

I was intrigued and took a trip downtown to check it out.

In 1913, William T. Whiteway, the same architect who designed the Sun Tower, created a four-storey brick residential building at 31 West Pender Street that was known as the Palmer Rooms. Over the years, it was called the Pender Hotel and the Wingate Hotel. Oddly, the building was formally recognized as one of Canada's Historic Places in 1994.

In fact, all that's left of the building is the front facade. The hotel is owned and operated by the Vancouver Native Housing Society, and they've done an impressive job of repurposing the building's old bones.

Judy Graves, who spent thirty-three years employed by the City of Vancouver, representing the marginalized and homeless people of the Downtown Eastside, was at the official sod-turning ceremony prior to the opening in 2012. She tells me that at the ceremony, two Indigenous elders spent a couple of hours smudging the basement foundation with sage. The cleansing ritual seems to have worked, because Skwachàys—the name for the area at the head of Vancouver's False Creek and pronounced "squatch eyes"—has a safe and welcoming feel.

The building provides twenty-four suites for artists and eighteen hotel rooms, each designed by an Indigenous artist to reflect a different theme, with suite names such as the Hummingbird, the Moon and the Northern Lights.

Included in the building is a traditional longhouse on the roof topped off by the *Dreamweaver Pole*—a forty-foot (twelve-metre) totem pole—as well as a sweat lodge, smudge room and artists' workshop. On the first floor is an Indigenous-run art gallery.

Skwachàys Lodge, 2020.

Courtesy Nathan Mawby

I say oddly because the place was a dump. The hotel was used as a repository for stolen property, and there were rumours of a meth lab, of involvement with a well-known criminal organization and of a connection to the serial killer Robert Pickton. The hotel had witnessed a lot of depravity and violence over the years, and, apparently, there wasn't much of it left worth saving.

THE WING SANG BUILDING

Yip Sang with children and family members in front of 51 East Pender Street, ca. 1890s.

Vancouver Archives
2008-010.4050

In 2006, I wrote a feature for *Marketing Magazine* on real estate marketer Bob Rennie and his move into Chinatown. Just two years before, Bob paid $1 million for the Wing Sang Building. He bought it sight unseen and didn't go inside for the first six months. "People think I'm crazy," he told me. "Do you want to go for a walk around inside? It's scary."

And it was—in a dilapidated, kind of fascinating way—and had clearly been abandoned for years. I followed Bob and his constantly ringing cellphone into the bowels of the building. When we came to a boarded-up door, Bob looked around, rolled up his expensive shirtsleeves and found a shovel to lever off the bar. Then we were climbing up six flights of stairs, past rattraps, broken windows and old stoves.

The original building, a two-storey Italianate structure, went up in 1889, back when the population of Vancouver was around 15,000 and extremely hostile to the Chinese. But even at a time when racism was rampant, Yip Sang became a successful businessman who operated an import-export business, a bank and a travel agency and sold everything from Chinese silks and curios to opium—which was legal until 1908. He added a third storey in 1901, and in 1912, a six-storey building went up across the alley, connected by an elevated passageway to include a warehouse, a meeting place and a floor for each of Yip Sang's three wives and their twenty-three children. Because there were so many offspring, they were each given a number in order of their birth.

Henry Yip, son of Kew Mow, third son of Yip Sang's first wife, was born in 1917 on the fourth floor of the building. He was only ten years old when his grandfather died, but when I talked to Henry in 2006, he told me he remembered Yip Sang as a "disciplinarian," who "used to sit beside a potbelly stove next to the doorway at the front of the building, smoking his pipe and watching everybody go in and out." Yip Sang had a strict curfew and would lock out family members who weren't home by ten p.m.

Shortly after my tour, Bob Rennie spent $10 million to turn the back of the building into a private gallery space to house his massive art collection—reputedly the third-largest private art collection in Canada. He left the original Chinese schoolroom untouched and put a neon sign that says "EVERYTHING IS GOING TO BE ALRIGHT" on the building's rooftop garden. Bob regularly holds free public tours of the building and art gallery, and at one point it became a satellite gallery for the Royal BC Museum with an exhibit of works by a young Emily Carr.

ABOVE Yip Sang and family members in front of 51 East Pender Street, ca. 1902.

Vancouver Archives 2008-010.4054

RIGHT The Wing Sang Building in 2020.

Eve Lazarus photo

THE SAM KEE SPITE HOUSE

The Sam Kee Building is considered the narrowest commercial building in the world.

Vancouver Archives Bu P255.7, 1936

When I first heard the term "spite house," I thought it was a style of architecture named after its designer—you know, "Oh, that's a Frank Lloyd Wright house" or an "Arthur Erickson house" or a "John Spite house." Turns out, it's far more interesting.

A spite house is built to piss somebody off. It's a permanent way to give city hall the finger or have the last word with that neighbour who has the annoying dog.

You can find plenty of examples of spite houses online. One dates back to 1716, when a man, upset by his small share of the family's estate in Massachusetts, built a house just tall enough to block the view from his two brothers' houses. More recently, in 2003, a Georgia man's plan to build a porch on his house was thwarted by the local historical preservation commission. In retaliation, the man painted the house bright green with purple dots.

Vancouver has a couple of spite houses of its own. The late John Davis and his family started buying up and renovating dilapidated Queen Anne and Edwardian houses along West Tenth Avenue in the early 1970s. Years ago, John gave me a tour of his properties and pointed out two Edwardian houses that touched each other. Turns out, this was intentional and came about as the result of a feud. Two women came over to Vancouver from England and had the house at 150 West Tenth built right on the property line. "That didn't offend the building code in 1907—if they even had such a thing—but it infuriated the owner of the property at 148, and he built his house the next year right up against their house in order to block the view out of the bay window on the side of 150, which he certainly achieved," said John.

Vancouver's 1913 Sam Kee Building at 8 West Pender Street is our most famous spite house. In the early 1900s, Chang Toy owned the Sam Kee Company, and one of his properties was a building at the corner of Pender and Carrall Streets on a standard thirty-foot (nine-metre) lot. Around 1911, the city expropriated part of his land when they decided to widen Pender Street. Toy was left with a sliver of dirt. To spite the officials, Toy built a steel-framed

three-storey structure with the ground floor measuring less than five feet (1.5 metres), with bay windows stretching out from the top floor. He also added a basement and opened a barbershop and bathhouse under the sidewalk.

As the neon sign out front attests, this slender building has been home to Jack Chow Insurance since 1986.

LEFT The Sam Kee Building, 8 West Pender Street.
Eve Lazarus photo, 2020

RIGHT The Sam Kee building, 8 West Pender Street.
Neil Whaley collection

THE DUPONT STREET DEPOT

If you're walking around Chinatown, you'll likely notice the four-storey brick building at the corner of East Pender and Columbia Streets, now home to the Vancouver Film School. But if you were to take a stroll down the 100 block of East Pender in the early years of the twentieth century, you would actually be on busy Dupont Street and you'd be quite likely to find visitors from the United States disembarking at the Vancouver, Westminster and Yukon Railway depot. Several hundred people came here to see the first fast train leave for Seattle on March 20, 1905, and cross the new trestle bridge that connected the north and south sides of False Creek. The last train to ever leave this depot departed on May 31, 1917, and the building was later turned into a Chinese restaurant. The last and most famous tenant was the storied Marco Polo nightclub.

Vancouver, Westminster and Yukon Railway depot on what was once Dupont Street (now East Pender Street), 1915.

Vancouver Archives PAN N100A

THE LOST SCRAPBOOKS FROM THE MARCO POLO

Tom Carter is a Vancouver artist, musician and collector, and I would bet he knows more about early Vancouver theatre than anyone else alive.

In 2017, he came across the "lost" scrapbooks from the Marco Polo restaurant. "The Marco Polo was one of Vancouver's legendary nightclubs," says Tom. "In the 1960s, it was considered one of the 'big three,' along with the Cave on Hornby and Isy's Supper Club on Georgia. While posters, cards and ephemera are pretty common from the Cave and Isy's, the Marco Polo has long been shrouded in mystery."

There have been rumours over the years that Marco Polo manager and part owner Victor Louie kept scrapbooks of the business and its clientele. Tom says they became fabled objects among a few serious collectors who had been hunting for them for years. Collectors are an obsessive lot who buy their memorabilia from second-hand stores, booksellers, heritage fairs and auctioneers. These dealers buy much of their stock from pickers—people who comb through back alleys and Dumpsters looking for treasure in other people's trash.

One of these pickers was rummaging through the garbage behind a Chinatown warehouse when he pulled out two scrapbooks from the Marco Polo. Thinking they might have some value, he sold them to a dealer. The books were full of photos of performing musicians and chorus girls. There were menus and handbills and letters from clients. Glued into the book was the script that Harvey Lowe—world-class yo-yo champion, owner of the Smilin' Buddha Cabaret and a staple of the Chinatown entertainment scene—used to emcee the opening show. There was

The interior of the Marco Polo nightclub.

Tom Carter collection

even a handwritten list of every act that played the club from 1964 to 1968. The scrapbooks told the story of the Marco Polo from the time the Louie brothers took over the Forbidden City restaurant in 1959 and renamed it, through to 1983, when they closed down the Chinatown nightclub and moved to North Vancouver.

Tom happened to drop by the dealer the day after he received the scrapbooks. Tom was horrified when he found that the dealer planned to dismantle the books and sell off the parts. It would have destroyed their historical value. So he bought everything.

Todd Wong's dad, Bill, and Victor Louie were friends, and Todd spent a large chunk of his childhood at the restaurant. "My father was the sign writer, and he painted many of the show cards as well as the big orange dragon on the Columbia Street side of the restaurant," says Todd. "I remember seeing the Platters, the Mills Brothers, and the Fifth Dimension there.

Dad would bring home stickers that said 'Pat Paulsen for President' [referring to the American comedian]. One evening when my dad was painting, I remember him asking if the name 'Ronstadt' was spelled correctly."

Todd was there the day the restaurant closed down. "It was a sad day," he says. "We sat there with Victor, and he said we could take any of the decorations, except the large wooden dragon carving which had already been sold."

Before the building could be destroyed in 1983, heritage advocate Arthur Irving made a deal with the demolition crew and pried eighty-eight bricks off the wall that still had the original railway sign "V.W. & Y. R^{Y} TO TRAINS" printed on it in black letters. He had the bricks mounted in a box to preserve them and, in doing so, saved one of the few pieces that remain of the Vancouver, Westminster and Yukon Railway that operated between 1904 and 1908. After Arthur died in 2018, Tom was helping clear out his house when he came across the sign and the blueprints for the Great Northern Railway's Union Station that was built in 1917. "We found them in Arthur's basement, in a bathtub salvaged from the 1916 Hotel Vancouver," says Tom.

The brick sign and the blueprints are now with the West Coast Railway Association in Squamish. The bathtub is in Arthur's next-door neighbour's garden.

ABOVE The China Doll dancers at the Marco Polo nightclub.
Tom Carter collection

LEFT Heritage advocates Tom Carter and Arthur Irving with the vintage railway sign in 2012.
Andrew Martin photo

RIGHT A menu from the Marco Polo nightclub.

Tom Carter collection

BELOW A 1968 talent list from the Marco Polo nightclub.

Tom Carter collection

Marco Polo

Food from the Far East
to meet western tastes

喜臨門酒家

90 Pender St. E. Vancouver 4, B.C.

FEB 15 – FEB 24 – THE GOSPEL J...
" 29 – MAR 9 – NINA SIMONE...
MAR. 25 – " 30 – PAT PAULSEN...
APR 1 – APR. 6 – SAMMY SHOR...
" 13 – " 20 – PONCIE PONCE...
" 22 – MAY 4 – EARL FATHA HINES (BUD...
                    PEMBERTON, BILL BASE...

MAY 8 – " 18 – THE 4 AMIGOS.
" 22 – JUNE 1 – RON ELIRAN & HALLIE SANDERS.
JUNE 5 – " 15 – THE SPICE RACQ
" 20 – " 29 – PAT WOODELL
JULY 3 – JULY 13 – GREG LEWIS & GUS CHRISTIE & VICKIE FRAZIER.
" 17 – " 27 – THE PAIR EXTRAORDINAIRE.
" 29 – AUG. 3 – SAM & DAVE REVUE
AUG. 5 – " 10 – JACKIE WILSON
" 14 – " 24 – THE MIDNIGHT HAZE
SEPT. 5 – SEPT. 14 – PETE BARBUTTI & ERNESTINE ANDERSON.
" 19 – " 28 – SKILES & HENDERSON & LAURA MADERO
OCT. 2 – OCT. 12 – CLARA WARD & THE WARD GOSPEL SINGERS
" 15 – " 26 – DICK JENSEN & THE IMPORTS,
" 30 – NOV. 9 – MAXINE BROWN.
NOV. 13 – DEC 7 – STEVE LOGAN & HIS HEROES (AUGIE COLON – BONGO...
" 27 – DEC 7 – ROBIN WILSON (DON HE'S PROTEGE')
                    PONCIE PONCE

JOE FORTES

In 1884, Trinidad-born Seraphim Joseph "Joe" Fortes was a seaman aboard the *Robert Kerr* sailing from Liverpool. When the ship ran aground in Burrard Inlet, and the crew was shipwrecked, Fortes decided to stay. He worked at Hastings Mill, tended bar and was a porter for a time, but after Vancouver burned to the ground in 1886, he started to teach kids to swim in English Bay—hundreds and hundreds of them. The official number of lives he saved is twenty-nine, but the actual count is estimated to be closer to 100. In 1901, Fortes was hired as the city's first lifeguard.

By 1904, Fortes had moved from his tent to a sweet little cottage at the foot of Gilford Street, right across from the Sylvia Hotel. When he heard that the city wanted to rid English Bay of private homes, his own included, he got permission from the mayor to put his house on skids and move it three blocks down Beach Avenue to the foot of Bidwell Street.

Fortes lived in his cottage by the water until his death in 1922. He was fifty-seven. His funeral was held at Holy Rosary Cathedral, and it was the most heavily attended in the city's history, with thousands of people spilling outside the packed church. In 1927, the people of Vancouver—many of them children—raised

Joe Fortes in front of his cabin at the foot of Bidwell Street, ca. 1910.

Vancouver Archives Bu P111, colourized by Mark Truelove, Canadian Colour

approximately $5,000 (the equivalent of about $75,000 in 2020) to build a memorial fountain in his honour. Charles Marega sculpted Fortes's face above a panel showing children wading in the water. It's inscribed with the words "little children loved him."

Fortes has a seafood restaurant and a library named for him. In 1986, the Vancouver Historical Society named him Citizen of the Century, and in February 2013, he was honoured with a stamp on the 150th anniversary of his birth.

Neither the city nor the parks board considered saving Fortes's home—perhaps moving it across the street to Alexandra Park, where it could have become a repository for the history of Joe Fortes, of the Black community in Vancouver and of the houses that once dotted the waterside of Beach Avenue. Instead it was burned to the ground—standard practice for demolition in the 1920s.

As for Alexandra Park, this lovely little green space by the water, was named English Bay Park until July 1911, when somebody thought it would be a good idea to rename it after Queen Alexandra, the wife of the dead king, Edward VII.

THE FORMER HOUSES OF BEACH AVENUE

Some years ago, when I first started researching Alvo von Alvensleben—one of my favourite characters from early-twentieth-century Vancouver history—I made several road trips to see how many of the buildings associated with him had withstood the bulldozer. Fortunately, many did. The financier and real estate investor's private home is now the old residence at Crofton House, a girls' school in Kerrisdale. The Wigwam Inn at Indian Arm, the Dominion Building on West Hastings Street, his hunting lodge in North Vancouver and houses that he built for employees in Pitt Meadows, Port Mann and Issaquah, Washington, still stand.

But I was intrigued by one that didn't.

In 1909, the city directory lists Alvensleben's home as 1409 Nicola Street, but when I looked for the address, I landed on the grassy promenade of Beach Avenue with nary a house in sight.

A trip to the library and session with the microfiche confirmed that around the turn of the twentieth century, the waterside of Beach Avenue was lined with more than thirty houses, bookended by the Englesea Lodge and what's now the Burrard Street Bridge. Some were fine old ivy-covered manors, others were more like Joe Fortes's rustic cabin at the foot of Bidwell Street. The city directory showed that 1409 Nicola was still there in 1950.

That year, a *Vancouver Sun* article with the headline "English Bay Drive to Become Reality" explained why: "Vancouver park commissioners will take aggressive steps this month to start on their 20-year dream to make Beach Avenue a panoramic marine drive from English Bay to Crystal Pool."[1]

In 1926, the Vancouver Town Planning Commission hired Harland Bartholomew, an American urban planner, to design a blueprint for Vancouver's growth. The 300-plus-page book was the catalyst behind divesting the shoreline of bricks and mortar. The first part of the plan involved the city expropriating fourteen houses in 1929 to make way for a pleasure drive. But the Depression and then the Second World War got in the way, and the houses became city-owned rentals for the next two decades. "Park commissioners are expected to ask the city in the next few weeks for authority to start tearing down two houses a year, beginning at English Bay and working westward until all are gone," went the article.

The parks board got its way until the only holdout was the Englesea Lodge.

Englesea Lodge and the houses along the waterside of Beach Avenue, taken from the Sylvia Hotel in 1913.
Vancouver Archives 2013-002.1

THE LIFE AND DEATH OF THE ENGLESEA LODGE

The Englesea Lodge was a handsome six-storey, forty-five-suite brick apartment block faced with terracotta that was built in 1911 on the water at the edge of Stanley Park. It was the last holdout from a time when the waterside of Beach Avenue was lined with private homes. Legendary lifeguard Joe Fortes lived in a cottage at the foot of Bidwell, and the English Bay Pier was a fixture of the West End.

The story of the Englesea Lodge spans half a century and features the parks board as villain, the city as wishy-washy and the Save-Englesea Committee as the pro-heritage group with the radical idea that the building was part of our history and could coexist perfectly well with the shoreline. Many of the tenants were seniors who had lived at the Englesea for decades, and protestors argued that with a vacancy rate of rental housing in

Vancouver at .2 percent, it made much more sense to retain these solid housing units that provided good middle- and low-cost housing. Sound familiar? In a letter to the editor in January 1980, a Mrs Le Nobel represented the opinion of many when she wrote: "Surely the park board does not intend to carry out so wasteful a scheme. How can they possibly justify tearing down this pleasant and useful building and replace it with grass? Grass! Our park board is obsessed with the stuff. Surely common sense will prevail."[2]

It didn't. The city paid $375,000 for the Englesea in 1967, and the battle to save it began. Council voted in 1979 to demolish the building. They issued eviction notices and locked up suites as they emptied. By the following year, well over half the apartments were still occupied, and there was talk from the city of investing $1.3 million to turn the building into seniors' housing. Suggestions were floated to convert the bottom floor into a tea room and extend the seawall around the building. But the parks board was determined to bulldoze English Bay back to sand and grass.

On Sunday, February 1, 1981, shortly before nine a.m., George Wright, a seventy-something caretaker, was working at the Englesea Lodge when he spotted fire coming from the building's basement storage area. "There was a big boom and the fire rushed out at me. It threw me back against the wall," he told a reporter.[3] Wright barely managed to escape through the rear basement door, but flames were already tearing up through two light shafts and up the elevator shaft and spreading through the floors of the six-storey building.

Retired Vancouver Fire Rescue Services captain Steve Webb was one of ninety firefighters called out that day to fight the blaze, with the help of an aerial ladder and thirteen trucks. There's no doubt in Steve's mind that it was arson. "The fire was not only obviously set in the basement next to the elevator shaft, but the fire 'operations and command' was also suspicious to us firefighters. The higher-ups wanted it to burn," he tells me. "Soon as we had a good grip on the seat of the fire, we were called out and the fire was allowed to rekindle and spread."

The fire left a smoke-blackened, gutted structure just two days before Vancouver City Council was scheduled to meet and discuss the Englesea's future. The day after the building burned down, Alderman Don Bellamy—who favoured the building's demolition—told a reporter that the fire was "like fate itself had taken hold." And then he added, "It's a hell of a shallow victory. If we're going to have our way, I hope to hell we don't have to fry people to do it."[4]

The Englesea Lodge, the Sylvia Hotel, the English Bay Pier and the houses along the waterside of Beach Avenue, 1913.
Vancouver Archives PAN NXV111

Paul Dixon was living on Comox Street when he awoke to the smell of smoke and the sound of sirens. He grabbed his camera and recorded the demise of the Englesea Lodge.

Paul Dixon photo, February 1, 1981

THE SYLVIA HOTEL

The Sylvia Court Apartments, ca. 1932.
Vancouver Archives 99-2632

In the ten years that Ross Dyck was the general manager at the Sylvia Hotel, he opened about 600 handwritten letters every year from fans of the children's book *Mister Got to Go*, mostly kids in grades one and two. And every year, he personally answered every one of them.

The *Mister Got to Go* books by author Lois Simmie and illustrator Cynthia Nugent about a cat that moved into the Sylvia Hotel are so popular, he says, that it wasn't uncommon to stumble across a busload of little tykes in the hotel lobby making a stop en route to the Vancouver Aquarium. "They force the bus driver to stop here so they can come in and find the cat," he said. " 'Course the cat hasn't been around for years, but we love the fact they still come."

The Sylvia, which celebrated its 100th anniversary in 2013, is a special kind of hotel. "When I first got here, I was horrified. I'd walk into the lobby at five-thirty a.m., and I'd see people walking around in their housecoats and slippers," says Ross. "But I can't think of any other hotel in Vancouver that can say that."

When the Sylvia was built as a seventy-unit apartment building in 1913—called the Sylvia Court—it was the tallest building in Vancouver, and it remained the tallest building in the West End until 1956. Named for the owner's daughter Sylvia Goldstein, the building was converted into a hotel in 1936 and received heritage designation in 1975.

Sylvia Hotel, 2020.
Eve Lazarus photo

Over the years, the hotel has hosted famous people such as Pierre Trudeau and Errol Flynn. Like a good hotel manager, Ross doesn't like to name his famous guests, but he was comfortable telling me that singer-songwriters Jane Siberry and Jennifer Warnes are both regulars.

One of Ross's favourite recollections involves the time a woman in her nineties came to stay at the hotel for a night. Her mother had stayed at the Sylvia years before, and she showed Ross the invoice. In those days, two nights' accommodation, two breakfasts and seven phone calls came to $7.14. When the woman checked out the next morning, Ross charged her $7.14.

In 2012, he says, the Sylvia hosted a fifth-generation wedding. The first family member was married there in 1913.

Ross, whose job was a bit like being mayor of a small town, says that the best part was that, in all the years that he worked at the Sylvia, he never had the same day twice.

ENGLISH BAY
PIER
(1908-39)

For three decades, a massive pier reached out across English Bay from the foot of Gilford Street.

English Bay Pier and English Bay, ca. 1912.
Vancouver Archives 71-17

PETER PANTAGES AND THE POLAR BEAR SWIM

On January 1, 2020, the Polar Bear Swim celebrated its 100th anniversary. It was by far the biggest year ever, with about 7,000 people hitting the water of English Bay. Being an Aussie, I really don't get the appeal of plunging into frigid salty water, but I do love the history behind this crazy local tradition.

Peter Pantages started the Polar Bear Swim in 1920, a year or so after he arrived in Vancouver from Andros, Greece, via New York, Chicago and Seattle. Peter worked at his uncle Alexander's Pantages Theatre on Hastings Street, and he'd swim at English Bay at least once every day. Soon, nine friends joined him on the daily dip. They

Tony, Lisa and Basil Pantages, Herb Capozzi and Tony Ferraro at the Polar Bear Swim, January 1, 1978.

Vancouver Sun, *Bill Keay photo*

became the first official members of the Polar Bear Club and kicked off the first Polar Bear Swim on Christmas Day, using the basement of the Sylvia Hotel to change and assemble. Under the constitution of the club, anyone who wanted to be president had to swim every day—no freezing rain, snow or sickness excused them. It's not surprising that Peter was voted president for the next fifty-one years.

When Peter swam alone on foggy Vancouver days, he'd find his way back to the beach by listening for the rattle of the streetcars at Denman and Davie. At other times, he'd leave a lighted red coal oil lantern to guide him back to shore. Peter's granddaughter Lisa Pantages became president of the Polar Bear Swim

TOP LEFT Spectators at the Polar Bear Swim, 1953.

Courtesy Lisa Pantages

BOTTOM LEFT Polar Bear Swim, in front of the English Bay Pier, 1935.

Courtesy Lisa Pantages

in 1990, after taking the mantle from her uncle Basil Pantages and long after the swim had moved to New Year's Day. The Pantages are still very much involved in the annual swim—more than fifty family members live in the Metro Vancouver and Sunshine Coast area—but these days, the parks board manages the event and Lisa is the swim's historian. "When you've been doing the swim for a number of years, you really feel the history in Vancouver, and I think that's such an important element of it," says Lisa. "It could be 1950 or 1980, and everybody has their own traditions, but when you come together you can really feel the magical aspects of the swim."

Traditions include a lot of dressing up. Over the years, there have been people dressed for a black-tie event, Vikings, Wonder Women, the Flash, wedding dresses, shark suits and pyjamas. Some years there have also been skydivers, scuba divers, water skiers and windsurfers.

In the early years, participants swam around the English Bay Pier. When that disappeared, there was a freestyle sprint to a red buoy 300 feet (100 metres) from shore. The water temperature has ranged from 36 to 48°F (2 to 9°C). In 1963, the parks board had to dig a trail through two feet of snow so that swimmers could reach the water.

In 1929, Peter opened the Peter Pan Cafe on Granville Street with his brothers Lloyd, Angelo and Alphonsos. The restaurant operated twenty-four hours a day and became a late-night haunt for out-of-town performers from the Cave or Isy's Supper Club. After the annual Polar Bear Swim, Peter would invite everyone back to his cafe for hot drinks and a turkey dinner or clambake and give out prizes ranging from bathing suits to a pound of butter during the war years.

Peter married Helen in 1930 and the couple spent their honeymoon on a steamship to California. Peter made a deal with the captain that would allow him to swim off the ship every day that conditions permitted. On the days when it wasn't possible, a steward would draw a cold saltwater bath and give him an official letter to that effect. A letter Lisa has on official Pacific Steamship Company letterhead and signed by the Captain, says: "This is to certify that, Peter Pantages, passenger on board this vessel from Wilmington, California to Seattle, Washington from November 30, 1930 to December 5, 1930 did during these dates, take daily cold salt water baths. Arrangements for these baths were made by Mr Pantages thru our Bath-Room Steward, and my investigation shows that these baths were taken daily without exception on the *Emma Alexander*."

Peter died in Hawaii in 1971, when his heart gave out. He was swimming, of course. Over the course of his life he made at least 18,000 daily swims.

1 Certificates of participation are handed out every year at the Polar Bear Swim.

Lisa Pantages collection

2 Polar Bear swimmers diving off English Bay Pier.

Courtesy Lisa Pantages

3 Diamond Ice truck at the Polar Bear Swim.

Courtesy Lisa Pantages

4 Polar Bear Swim, undated.

Courtesy Lisa Pantages

IVY GRANSTROM: QUEEN OF THE POLAR BEARS

Ivy Granstrom participated in seventy-six consecutive Polar Bear Swims. She began in 1928, as a sixteen-year-old, which, incidentally, was the year of the chilliest swim on record with a water temperature of just 36°F (2°C).

Legally blind since she was three weeks old, Granstrom became a remarkable athlete and was an unstoppable force even after a car accident left her with a severe back injury at age sixty. To rehabilitate, she started walking, then jogging, then running right into the record books of Masters track competitions.

In 1994, Granstrom broke five records: two at the Pan Am Masters Championships and three at the World Masters Games in Australia. In 1980, the sixty-eight-year-old was running eighteen miles (thirty kilometres) a week with Paul Hoeberigs, who would guide her by voice, each holding on to the end of a cloth band. When she wasn't running or swimming she liked to curl, do carpentry work, garden and ski, depending on the time of year. Granstrom was named Sport BC Athlete of the Year in 1982, appointed a Member of the Order of Canada in 1988 and inducted into the Terry Fox Hall of Fame in 2001.

She died in April 2004, four months after completing her last Polar Bear Swim.

THE SIMPSON BLOCK

The Simpson Block's replacement.
Mark Dunn photo, 2020

Went I first came to Vancouver in the 1980s, we used to hang out at the Bayside Lounge in the odd silo-shaped building at Denman and Davie Streets. Until I saw a historical photo, I didn't realize that it had replaced an elegant four-storey apartment building with distinctive diamond-patterned brickwork that stood at that corner until 1976.

Zach and Will Simpson, a couple of entrepreneur brothers who bought a ton of property along Beach Avenue in the late 1800s, built the Simpson Block in 1912. They also constructed the boathouse across the road and rented out rowboats.

The Simpson Block was built over a stream on a sandy site. Charles Bentall, who went on to head up Dominion Construction, did the steel frame on the building over deep foundations. In it, there were thirteen apartments and a drugstore at retail level. John McMahon ran the corner drugstore from 1926 until his retirement in 1959. "We used to buy bathing suits—navy blue cotton made in Germany," he told a reporter in 1973. "We'd land them in the drugstore at 20 cents and sell them for a buck. They came in four sizes—small, medium, large and children's. I can remember those bathing suits hanging on people yet. They looked terrible."[5]

By 1930, the Depression was in full force and times were tough, but people still came to English Bay. "Whole families came out from Alberta and Saskatchewan and stayed two and three weeks all lined up and down Davie and along Beach," said McMahon. "You'd find up to 20 people in a house with one bathroom. They talk about density now. You should have seen the numbers of people in those rooming houses in the Depression." He remembered the old English Bay Pier with the pavilion

Simpson Block,
ca. 1975.

*Vancouver Archives
447-370*

that served as concert hall, dance hall, tea spot and roller-skating rink. "Occasionally girls would jump off the stands hoping to bring about an abortion," said McMahon. "Mostly they just broke a leg. There was a grocery store next to the Sylvia Hotel. The fellow would phone me and I'd call up the ambulance."[6]

By 1972, the Sands Motor Hotel, which then owned the building, was forging ahead with plans for a twenty-three-storey hotel with a 400-seat beer parlour. The parks board was opposed to the project, saying it would create an impossible traffic and parking situation. The drugstore left the Simpson Block in 1972 and a young guy named Heath Beggs renovated

the space for his clothing and crafts business, the English Bay Trading Company. He gathered wood from the beach and made window display boxes from the wood salvaged from an 1896 New Westminster house that had been demolished. "We're hoping that our store and the others coming into the block will prevent the building from being torn down," he told a *Vancouver Sun* reporter.[7] No such luck. The tower never came to be, and the building was sold to Royal Oak Holdings. The plan was to build luxury units in a building patterned after Montreal's Habitat 67 model community housing complex. Clearly, that didn't happen—now the silo dominates that busy corner of the West End.

MORTON PARK

In 1907, more than 100 years before the famous laughing statues appeared at English Bay, the Imperial Roller Skating Rink opened in Morton Park. Roller skating was surging in popularity at the time. The rink was housed in a big wood-framed building with a huge tower that looked out over Beach Avenue and boasted the largest skating floor on the continent.

The first game of polo on roller skates at the rink took place on January 22, 1908. The following summer the rink turned into a theatre, hosting a production of Gilbert and Sullivan's *H.M.S. Pinafore* by the Imperial Opera Company. The building turned back into a skating rink for a time, and then in January 1914 it burned to the ground.

Soon afterward, Almond's Ice Cream Store set up their operations in Morton Park. The little store was an offshoot of city alderman Henry Elston Almond's successful manufacturing business. He died in 1929 and left an estate worth $269,000 made up of ice-cream shares and real estate. Almond Park in Kitsilano is named for him.

Love them or hate them, and I do love them, the laughing sculptures in English Bay are here to stay. Designed by Yue Minjun, each of the fourteen bronze statues stands more than nine feet (three metres) tall and weighs more than 500 pounds (226 kilograms). They were installed in 2009 as part of the Vancouver Biennale, a program that puts international art in public spaces. The inscription carved into the concrete reads, "May this sculpture inspire laughter playfulness and joy in all who experience it." To give credit where it's due, *A-maze-ing Laughter* is now a permanent exhibit because Lululemon athletic wear founder Chip Wilson forked over US$1.5 million to keep the sculptures in the public domain—perhaps because he can see them from across the water at his Kitsilano mansion, which regularly tops the list of British Columbia's most expensive houses.

TOP English Bay and the Imperial Roller Skating Rink, ca. 1909.

Vancouver Archives Be P39.3

MIDDLE Almond's Ice Cream Store, ca. 1920.

Vancouver Archives 99-3097, colourized by Mark Truelove, Canadian Colour

BOTTOM *A-maze-ing Laughter,* a collection of fourteen bronze sculptures, was installed in Morton Park in 2009 as part of the Vancouver Biennale.

Eve Lazarus photo, 2020

CRYSTAL POOL

Joe Fortes taught hundreds of children how to swim in English Bay. If the much-loved lifeguard were still alive when Crystal Pool opened in July 1929, it's hard to imagine that the parks board would have gotten away with separate swim days—six days for white people, one day for "negroes and orientals"[8]—segregating their mostly young customers for the next seventeen years.

This saltwater pool at Sunset Beach was built as part of a swanky private club called the Connaught Beach Club. In addition to the pool, there were plans to include tennis, badminton and squash courts, Turkish baths for men and women, a beauty parlour, a barbershop, a roof garden and a ballroom. But the operators ran out of money and the contractors finished only the pool in return for shares in lieu of cash.

The city bought the land in 1939 and the parks board held the lease. The pool had bled money during the Depression, and some of the stunts to bring in customers included watching George Burrows, superintendent of beaches and parks, leap off the diving board tied in a gunny sack as part of his underwater-escape act. Manager Gordon Ross was talked into diving through the air to hit a ring of flame on the water, while swim coach Percy Norman would wrestle contenders on a platform until one fell into the water. Another draw was throwing 1,000 pennies into the pool and inviting kids to dive for them. The kids would later return them to the pool coffers by buying sweets at the concession stand. On Saturdays, a fifteen-cent admission got kids a hot dog, a Coke and bus fare home.

In 1945, twenty-one-year-old Vivian Jung was stopped from getting the life-saving certificate she needed to join the Vancouver School Board as a full-time teacher. She wasn't allowed to swim in Crystal Pool with the white folks. Her students and colleagues refused to go to the pool without her, and the segregation rule was finally abolished. Jung became the first Chinese Canadian teacher hired by the VSB and taught at Vancouver's Tecumseh Elementary School for thirty-five years. In 2014, the year she died, Jung Lane was named for her. Fittingly, the lane runs right by Sunset Beach.

In 1966, Harry McPhee, head of the Seahorse Swim Club, went to war with the parks board in an effort to save the pool from demolition for competitive swimmers, even though the facility was aging and losing money. "Perhaps it was a fluke by the builders in the first place, but it's the right width, the right length, the right everything," he told a reporter. "It may not look all that glamorous, but it's got something of the Stradivarius about it."[9] McPhee lost. Crystal Pool was demolished, though Vancouver gained the Aquatic Centre, which opened in 1974.

THE SS *ESSINGTON*

For most of the 1970s, the SS *Essington*, a sternwheeler that once plied the Skeena and Fraser Rivers, was turned into a seafood restaurant and moored under the Burrard Street Bridge next to Crystal Pool at Sunset Beach. Many people remember eating there after a swim and listening to local musicians, such as Wilmer Fawcett and Blaine Tringham, play jazz on Sundays. The restaurant became Horatio's in 1980 and reopened as Tommy Africa's in 1983. The sternwheeler is a distant memory, but its paddlewheel has lived on at the 'Ksan Historical Village and Museum in Hazelton since 1989.

FRITZ AUTZEN AND THE HIPPOCAMPUS

The Hippocampus at 1076 Denman Street, ca. 1960.

Fritz Autzen photo, courtesy Chris Stiles

Fritz Autzen, a baker from Neukölln, Germany, moved his family to BC in 1954. Within five years he had saved up enough money working as a cook to take over the Hippocampus, a fish and chip shop at 1076 Denman Street.

His business card has the shop's opening hours of eleven a.m. to ten p.m., Tuesday to Sunday. "I remember the first few years my dad had the business he never closed for holidays because he was afraid that somebody else would come and take his customers," says Fritz's daughter, Chris Stiles.

When he wasn't working, Fritz loved to take photos. Chris and her older brother, Michael, went to Lord Roberts Elementary School. Because Monday was the only day the store closed, Fritz would grab his camera, take the kids out of school and hit Stanley Park to pick huckleberries at Lost

TOP Fritz Autzen invented the torpedo sandwich.
Courtesy Chris Stiles

BOTTOM A great shot of the buried houses from above, with early construction of Denman Place Mall left of frame, ca. 1965.
Fritz Autzen photo, courtesy Chris Stiles

Lagoon, or Chinatown to eat at the Marco Polo. In summer, the kids would wait for the diving barge and Big Bertha, the floating slide to come in at English Bay.

Chris still has Fritz's immigration papers from when her father entered Canada a few months ahead of his family in 1954. His net worth at the time was $226 and included his clothes (valued at $160), a pair of binoculars and his Teco camera.

Fritz invented the torpedo sandwich, a forerunner to the giant submarine sandwich, and garlic vinegar to put on your fish and chips.

The house and a retail store are still there in a row along Denman Street near Davie, one of the four buried houses on that block. These houses were built in the early 1900s, but a look through the city directories shows the storefronts weren't added until the 1940s. By the end of that decade, Harry Almas, who owned the King Neptune Seafoods restaurant in New Westminster and, in 1959, North Vancouver's Seven Seas restaurant at the foot of Lonsdale Avenue, bought 1076 Denman and added three apartments. The Hippocampus opened in 1953. Fritz and his wife, Herta, moved into Harry and Eva Almas's apartment and managed the other two apartments in return for a break on the rent.

The family lived above the store from 1959 to 1968. That year, they moved to Richmond and Fritz opened the Seahorse Cafe. When Fritz died in 1981, he left more than 1,000 slides.

VANCOUVER'S BURIED HOUSES

The first time I really noticed one of Vancouver's buried houses was when I came across a painting by author and historian Michael Kluckner in his book *Vanishing Vancouver: The Last 25 Years*. I googled the Kitsilano address and was astonished to find that the house was still there at 2052 West Fourth Avenue, lurking behind an ice-cream parlour. "It's a 1905 house with a 1927 addition on the front," Michael tells me. "Over the years it has housed a dry cleaner, a build-it-yourself radio shop and a poster store catering to the hippies in nearby rooming houses. It was nicknamed the Rampant Lion, after the tenants' rock band."

Some homeowners on commercial streets started building shops in the front yards of their houses in the 1920s, a practice that increased in the '30s as a way to ride out the Depression. These early home-based businesses ranged from bakeries and meat markets to cigarette shops

Buried houses on Denman and Davie Streets, 1928.
Vancouver Archives Str N267.1

and barbers, shoe repairs, groceries and bookstores.

"A typical Vancouver commercial street, right up until the 1970s, was a mix of shops, a few apartment buildings and houses," says Michael. "Houses, just like other buildings, adapt or die, and there is not a lot of old Vancouver, at least on the commercial streets, that can adapt to the new reality of land prices, taxes, the desire to densify and the changing retail landscape."

Another buried house at 1812 West Fourth, near Burrard, has been a butcher's, a used furniture shop, a grocery store and a cafe. Now it's painted bright green and hosts Canna Clinic marijuana dispensary. Gregory Melle tells me that it was his late brother's head shop in the early '70s. Later, it became an Indian restaurant. "I was amused to see last year that it had reverted to the same business for which it was infamous in my brother's day," Gregory says.

Numbers Cabaret, the gay nightclub at 1042 Davie Street, hides a buried house behind it. It's been added to, and there's a noticeable bump where the new section joins the original house and forms part of the club.

There are still a number of buried houses around Vancouver, especially in Kitsilano, South Granville, Commercial Drive and Davie Street. You just have to look hard to find them.

TOP Michael Kluckner stands in front of a row of three buried houses, built between 1921 and 1937, at Renfrew near First Avenue in Vancouver.

Christine Allen photo, 2020

BOTTOM Buried houses on Denman and Davie Streets, 2016.

Gregory Melle photo

MAXINE
AND THE BEAUTY
SCHOOL

John Atkin is a well-known civic historian, author and heritage consultant who regularly leads tours around the West End. One of his stops is the JJ Bean coffee shop on Bidwell Street, which sits behind the facade of what was once Maxine Beauty School.

John says the most common question he's asked is if there was ever a tunnel that connected sugar baron Benjamin Tingley Rogers's mansion Gabriola on Davie Street with a bootlegging operation and brothel situated in Maxine's. "Apart from the general absurdity of the idea—the elevation change between Gabriola and Maxine's would have made a tunnel an incredibly expensive engineering feat—Maxine's was built in 1936—long after prohibition ended in BC and three years after it was repealed south of the border," says John. "There was no need for a bootlegging operation, let alone tunnels in the building, and the idea that a tunnel was used by sugar magnate B.T. Rogers to access a bordello from his home makes no sense because Rogers died in 1918."

But while Maxine MacGilvray may not have been a madame, or a female Al Capone, it turns out she was quite enterprising and built a series of successful businesses in Vancouver and Seattle.

After he spent some time with the 1940 US Census, Skagit County marriage licences, immigration records, city directories and the *Vancouver World* newspaper, John found that MacGilvray's name first pops up in 1914 in connection with beauty products sold by Spencer's department store, where she gave presentations on skin care.

"Maxine started with a hair salon in the 600 block of Dunsmuir, opened her second

ABOVE LEFT Maxine Beauty School on Bidwell Street, 1936.
Vancouver Archives 99-4477

ABOVE RIGHT In 2016, the City of Vancouver named a street for Maxine MacGilvray: Maxine Lane runs from Burrard to Bidwell Street.
Eve Lazarus photo, 2020

RIGHT John Atkin, civic historian, talking to a tour group in August 2014 about the history of the building.
Courtesy Vancouver Heritage Foundation

location in the 1920s on the ground floor of a house at 1211 Bidwell Street and followed this with the opening of the Maxine College of Beauty Culture next door," says John. "She manufactured her own beauty products in a small factory on East Georgia Street called the Max Chemical Company."

Newspaper articles and ads have her as "Mlle Maxine"—even though she was born in Wisconsin.

In 1928, Maxine MacGilvray, then thirty-six, married her twenty-six-year-old apprentice, Ivor Ewan Bebb, and they renamed the business the Max-Ivor Company. They hired an architect to design a Mission Revival building to replace the older building on Bidwell. According to a story in the *Edmonton Journal* in July 1937, MacGilvray, president and founder, was a graduate of the University of California and had a degree in pharmacy and chemistry. "She is an authority on Electro-therapy and Bacteriology and a graduate in science of cosmetology, and carries the master degree of MSC," went the article. "Mr Max-Ivor is vice-president and business manager, chief chemist, instructor in salesmanship and personal efficiency."[10]

MacGilvray was obviously an extremely astute businesswoman, not only surviving through the Depression but also expanding her business. A story in the *Vancouver Sun* in September 1938 said the main floor of the beauty school had an auditorium that could seat more than 200 students, a haircutting room, a lecture stage and several classrooms.

When the school closed in 1942, the building was converted into the Maxine Apartments, and she and Bebb opened the Max-Ivor Motel in Seattle. MacGilvray died in 1952, but her name continued on the new business: the Maxine Hotel.

The Maxine Hotel gained some notoriety in 1960 when six carloads of Vancouver police and FBI men surrounded the hotel one morning to arrest Joseph Corbett Jr., age thirty-two, who was on the FBI's Ten Most Wanted list. Corbett had been on the run since 1955, after escaping from a California jail where he was serving time for the murder of a US Air Force sergeant. He was wanted for the kidnapping and murder of wealthy Colorado brewer Adolph Coors III. Corbett, one of the biggest arrests in Vancouver's history, probably could have spent much longer on the lam but decided to rent a flashy red convertible with Manitoba licence plates and park it out front of the Maxine Hotel. He went peacefully with the officers and left a .380 ACP calibre Llama pistol on the chesterfield in his room.

In 2016, the City of Vancouver named a street for Maxine MacGilvray: Maxine Lane runs from Burrard Street to Bidwell Street.

B.C. BINNING'S MISSING MURALS

B.C. Binning wasn't just an important artist; as a teacher, he influenced architects such as Arthur Erickson, Ron Thom and Fred Hollingsworth. His tiled murals are still outside the BC Hydro Building (now the Electra Building) on Burrard Street, as well as in and outside his West Vancouver house, which was designated a heritage building in 1999 and a National Historic Site in 2001.

What you can't see are the murals that he created for the old Vancouver Public Library, or the mural he created in 1956 to wrap around the CKWX building on Burrard Street that was replaced by a twenty-storey condo tower just thirty-three years later.

The University of British Columbia came up with most of the $8,000 needed to rescue a twenty-four-foot (7.3-metre) section of the CKWX mural, while Andrew Todd, a Vancouver conservator, was charged with prying Binning's blue, green and yellow mosaic off the wall, tile by tile, and placing it on a rolled canvas for storage at UBC. "Oh my God, it was tough to save," Todd told me. "It was an abstract arrangement of one-inch glass tiles from Venice, much like his mural on the BC Hydro Building. And it was huge, maybe twenty feet by ten feet [six by three metres] in sections." The saved section of the mural was to be installed on a proposed studio-resources building, which was to house the university's fine arts program. The building was never built, and the mural has apparently disappeared.

B.C. Binning's mural still decorates the old BC Hydro Building, which was converted into condos in the early 1990s.
Doris Fiedrich photo, 2017

THE GARDEN FAMILY

If you're in the market for a $30,000 Hublot watch, a cute little pair of diamond studs for five grand to go with that Prada bag or some private wealth management advice at the National Bank, then you are already familiar with the Carlyle at Alberni and Thurlow Streets. Luxury retail at street level and presumably luxury condos dispersed among its twenty storeys.

But before the high-rise, and before Alberni Street became Vancouver's Rodeo Drive, that corner of the city housed tea merchants, feisty women's associations and one of the city's hottest nightspots.

The first to claim the corner were William and Mary Garden. They arrived in Vancouver with their two sons from Helensburgh, Scotland, via Liverpool and a cross-Canada train trip in April 1889. William opened Garden and Sons Wholesale Tea and Coffee on East Hastings Street, and five years later, the Garden family moved into their new home at the corner of Thurlow and Alberni Streets.

Vancouver's first lifeguard, Joe Fortes, taught the Garden kids to swim at nearby English Bay.

William died in 1897 and the business closed. William Junior worked at the Bay and played piano in the house band at the Lester Court ballroom on Davie Street (now Celebrities Nightclub). His brother, Jack, became a lumber broker with a passion for photography, and he documented the family's various activities—at the house, the rowing club and biking in Stanley Park.

The next resident of that corner was William Lamont Tait, a wealthy retired lumber baron and real estate tycoon who lived there from 1903 while Glen Brae, his Shaughnessy mansion was being built.

In 1911, a group of delegates representing twelve different women's associations formed the Vancouver Women's Building Ltd. They bought the house by selling 8,000 shares at twenty-five dollars each, because it wasn't until 1964 that married women in Canada could open bank accounts without their husband's signature, let along get a loan or a mortgage.

The house was turned into a ten-cents-a-day crèche for working mothers. Though the provision of child care wasn't exactly for compassionate reasons—the wealthy had a critical shortage of domestic help—it was certainly groundbreaking. The house had accommodation for twenty and an annex for up to twenty-one women in crisis.

The house quickly became too small for their needs, and the formidable Helen Gregory MacGill—BC's first female judge—spearheaded a campaign to raise the money for a new building. On September 30, 1926, a three-storey building opened and the old house was moved to the back of the property for use as offices and a meeting space.

The new building had a dining room, an auditorium with a stage and dance floor, a reading room, classrooms and an employment bureau. The various women's organizations occupied the building until the Second World War, when the Salvation Army moved in and then stayed for a decade. It changed hands a number of times until 1966, when it became the nightclub Oil Can Harry's for the next eleven years. "There was nothing quite like Oil Can Harry's in Vancouver at the time," writes Aaron Chapman in *Vancouver After Dark*. "The club featured two separate rooms—Harry's Go Go Room upstairs and Dirty Sal's Cellar downstairs—so the club could essentially host two acts and two different crowds at the same time." The club added a third room in 1969, notes Chapman.[11]

The Carlyle replaced the Thurlow Street building in 1989 and changed its address to Alberni Street.

1 William Garden shows off his new lawn mower at his house at 752 Thurlow Street, ca. 1890s.

John H. Garden photo, courtesy Catherine Falk

2 Vancouver Women's Building, 1927.

Vancouver Archives Bu N292

3 Oil Can Harry's, 1974.

Vancouver Archives 778-433

4 The Carlyle on Alberni Street.

Eve Lazarus photo, 2020

TOP Wootton Manor,
1221 Burnaby Street,
1956.
*Vancouver Archives
Bu P.508.64*

BOTTOM 1221
Burnaby Street.
*Eve Lazarus photo,
2020*

WEST END
HERITAGE

When the City of Vancouver waived the six-storey height limit for residential buildings in the 1950s, it caused a frenzy of demolition in the West End. The neighbourhood lost dozens of sturdy old Victorian, Queen Anne, Arts and Crafts and Craftsman houses built from first-growth timber and handcrafted stone, as well as the well-established gardens that surrounded them. Instead of being repaired and repurposed, these structures were replaced with ones made from inferior materials and with uninspiring architecture, such as boxy apartment buildings and unimaginative towers. The only evidence that the former houses ever existed are a few stone fences that dot the West End.

THE STUART BUILDING

The Stuart Building was a landmark that sat at the southeast corner of Georgia and Chilco Streets, marking the border between the city and Stanley Park from 1909 until its demise in 1982. It didn't have the elegance of the Birks Building, the grandeur of the second Hotel Vancouver or the presence of the Georgia Medical-Dental Building. It was simply a modest three-storey wood-frame building painted sky blue and capped with a turret. There was a store that rented bikes and a craft shop on the ground floor and accommodation above, and I imagine it was this simplicity that appealed to the many people who petitioned so hard to try and save it.

Macau billionaire Stanley Ho, a.k.a. "the King of Gambling," bought the Stuart Building and its lot in 1974 for $275,000. Ho offered to upgrade the building and give the city a thirty-year lease in exchange

for zoning incentives on another property, but in 1982, most Vancouver City Council members followed a suggestion from Alderman George Puil to "get rid of it for once and for all." The vote was 7–3, with Harry Rankin, Bruce Yorke, Bruce Eriksen, Warnett Kennedy, Don Bellamy and Nathan Divinsky voting for demolition. Mayor Mike Harcourt, Marguerite Ford and May Brown voted against.[12]

Angus McIntyre photographed the building in the 1970s, and he was there to record its untimely end at dawn one July morning, the earliness of the hour chosen presumably to get there before the protestors and avoid unpleasantness. Angus says that, at the time, Chilco was a through street from Beach Avenue. "The West End had no diverters or barriers or stop signs, for that matter. There was a stop sign at Georgia, and it was a legal but dicey left

turn to head to the Lions Gate Bridge," he says. "The cars on Chilco would back up all the way to Beach but were kept moving by a policeman. He also stopped all the traffic to let the trolley buses turn into and out of Chilco and Georgia."

Barb Wood painted the Stuart Building on the cover of a Vancouver centennial engagement calendar in 1986. After witnessing the demolition, she said: "We were told it was too frail to stand, so it should come down. When they drove the first bulldozer through it, the results were like a Bugs Bunny cartoon—the structure was so sound, that the machine left a bull-dozer shaped hole, side to side."[13]

TOP Stuart Building, ca. 1971.
Angus McIntyre photo

MIDDLE Demolishing the Stuart Building, 1982.
Angus McIntyre photo

BOTTOM The Stuart Building's replacement.
Eve Lazarus photo, 2020

THE HORSE SHOW BUILDING

Also known as the Stanley Park Armouries, the Horse Show Building was the largest building in Vancouver and, with the exception of Madison Square Garden, the largest of its kind in North America, when it opened in 1909. It had carriage rooms and harness rooms and 150 loose stall boxes, but it wasn't always used by horses. Canada's seventh prime minister, Sir Wilfrid Laurier, made a campaign speech there in 1910, and it became the home of various military units, including the Irish Fusiliers, the Medical Service Corps and the Royal Canadian Army Service Corps. The structure was made of wood, with a steel truss roof, and it burned to the ground in 1960. This prime piece of real estate on the edge of Stanley Park stayed empty until the Laguna Parkside—a twenty-three-storey condo building—opened in 2007.

Horse Show Building (Stanley Park Armouries), 1910.
Vancouver Archives Bu P554

DEVONIAN HARBOUR PARK

When I think of all the demolition and destruction that we've put Vancouver through over the last century, it amazes me that we still have Stanley Park. It's not from lack of trying, though—developers have been trying to chip away at it for years.

The name of the eleven-acre (4.5-hectare) green space along Coal Harbour at the Georgia Street entrance to Stanley Park known as Devonian Harbour Park has nothing to do with the area's Indigenous history, the land's connection to the Kanakas, the buildings that once dotted its landscape or the city, for that matter. The park was named for the Calgary-based Devonian Group of Charitable Foundations, which forked over $600,000 to develop the site to its present look in 1983.[14]

Kanaka was a term for Indigenous Hawaiians who came to Canada in the early 1800s to work in the fur trade for the Hudson's Bay Company. Most went home when their work was done, but some stayed, married Squamish women and settled in Coal Harbour. The area became known as Kanaka Ranch, or the cherry orchard, because of the many cherry trees that were planted there, alongside apple trees and berry bushes.

The city and the parks board wanted Stanley Park left as a wilderness retreat for the city's white working class and to be free to develop the land at Coal Harbour. By the 1900s they had successfully chased the Kanakas out of the area and over to the Mission Reserve in North Vancouver. And so, in 1911, with a population of around 100,000, Vancouver felt big enough to sustain a 10,000-seat arena, with the first

Denman Arena fire, August 1936.

Vancouver Archives 94-51, colourized by Mark Truelove, Canadian Colour

artificial ice in Canada. It was built by a couple of young guys from Victoria: brothers Frank and Lester Patrick (aged twenty-five and twenty-seven, respectively), who needed a home for their new Pacific Coast Hockey Association. This was huge. As a comparison, Rogers Arena, built in 1995, when the city's population was nearly 1.8 million, has a seating capacity of 18,910.

The Denman Arena sat at the northwest corner of Denman and Georgia Streets and hosted the New Westminster Royals, the Victoria Aristocrats and the Vancouver Millionaires hockey teams. In 1915, the Millionaires won the Stanley Cup—Vancouver's first and only—when they beat the Ottawa Senators in three straight games. But the arena was for much more than hockey. Jack Dempsey and James Braddock boxed there, Rudolph Valentino judged a beauty contest and Arthur Conan

Doyle, creator of Sherlock Holmes, gave a speech in the building. It was also used for public skating, curling, wrestling matches, military assemblies and musical performances.

Then, on August 20, 1936, just hours after 4,000 boxing fans watched Max Baer fight James Walsh, the building burned to the ground.

In 1927, the Patrick brothers had built the Denman Auditorium just to the south of the Denman Arena. The auditorium survived the 1936 fire, went through a few different owners and names and hosted everything from political rallies to orchestras, wrestling matches, dance marathons and a strange assortment of revivalists and faith healers from the United States. The Vancouver Symphony, Jack Benny, Danny Kaye, Nat King Cole, the Everly Brothers and Paul Anka all played the auditorium. The building was demolished in 1959 because the Queen Elizabeth Theatre was soon to open.

With the buildings gone, developers were eager to transform the area and build a hotel and condos. The first attempt came from a New York developer in the early 1960s. The second by a local outfit called Harbour Park Developments that bought the land in 1964 and proposed a $55 million development with fifteen towers ranging between fifteen and thirty-one storeys high. The third attempt was a plan by the Four Seasons Hotel chain to build a

RIGHT A peace sign garden at All Seasons Park, the proposed site of a Four Seasons Hotel near the entrance to Stanley Park, May 30, 1971.

Province, *Gordon Sedawie photo*

BELOW Rocking to the music of Country Joe and the Fish at Vancouver's first be-in at Ceperley Park, Easter Sunday, March 26, 1967.

Vancouver Sun, *Ken Oakes photo*

fourteen-storey hotel, three thirty-storey condo towers and a bunch of townhouses. This was during the destructive era when Mayor Tom Campbell (1967–72) and the Non-Partisan Association (NPA) were replacing swaths of heritage buildings with the Pacific Centre and Vancouver Centre malls, pushing for freeways that would knock out large parts of the city and lobbying for Project 200, a proposed waterfront redevelopment program that would have taken out most of the heritage buildings in Gastown.

On May 29, 1971, about 100 hippies and activists took over the site. The Stanley Park protesters planted maple trees and vegetables, dug a pond, installed children's playground equipment and called it All Seasons Park.

They stayed for nearly a year.

Joanne Gregoire looks back on that time proudly. Six months pregnant at the time, she was there at the beginning of the protest, with her partner and a counter-culture organization called Cool Aid founded by lawyer Ray Chouinard, Simon De Jong—who would later become a New Democratic Party MP in Saskatchewan—and Elmore Smalley. "Cool Aid was responsible for starting feed-ins, free medical clinics, the first food co-op and drop-in shelter crash pads," Joanne says. "We certainly were a force to be reckoned with, and so many programs that are in place today are a direct result of those times. I still feel very proud that to this day the land has been preserved and some of our hippie social legacies continue."

Mayor Tom Campbell issued a plebiscite, stacking the odds in his favour by only allowing property owners to vote to accept the Four Seasons' plan. He succeeded, and the city won the battle when they brought in backhoes on April 20, 1972, to knock all the shelters down. Fortunately, they lost the war, and the plan fell apart later that year when the federal government refused to hand over a crucial piece of land for the development. Five years later, the land was purchased by the City of Vancouver and annexed to Stanley Park.

One of the most popular features of the park is the bronze sculpture of the woman sitting on a park bench. She's searching through her bag, looking for the glasses that she's forgotten are on top of her head. One Valentine's Day, the woman was mysteriously joined by another bronze statue—that of early North Vancouver settler Walter M. Draycott. No one is saying how Walter got all the way to Stanley Park from his Lynn Valley bench, but he was returned without incident and bolted into place to stop him from wandering off again.

J. Seward Johnson bronze sculpture of a woman on a bench, 1975.

Eve Lazarus photo, 2020

JIMMY CUNNINGHAM AND THE STANLEY PARK SEAWALL

Next time you're walking along the Stanley Park seawall, spare a thought for James "Jimmy" Cunningham. The little Scotsman spent thirty-two years of his life heaving granite blocks weighing hundreds of pounds and built more than half of the 5.5-mile (nine-kilometre) wall.

Cunningham, who stood just five foot four (1.6 metres), immigrated to Vancouver in 1910. The building of the Stanley Park seawall started in 1917 and Cunningham became master stonemason for the parks board in 1931. His granddaughter Julia Flather Murrell says he would talk to her in Gaelic. During her nursing training, she would meet Cunningham at the seawall, and she remembers his gnarled, swollen hands. "His right hand was really quite swollen and almost deformed because of all the cutting," she says. "He never stopped working on the wall. They lowered him down on the rope at low tide. He chose the rock to be cut and then cut the rock down on the beach. He did all the work himself. And he was still doing that into his eighties."

Ron Gordon, who worked for Cunningham, told the *Vancouver Sun*, "One time when he was sick with pneumonia he got up and came down in his pyjamas because he figured we couldn't get along without him. The seawall was his whole life."[15]

Stuart Lefeaux, a civil engineer who retired in 1978 and died in 2011, masterminded much of the layout of the seawall. In 2007, he told me that most of the granite blocks came from the beach, the city streets and a stone quarry on Nelson Island along the Sunshine Coast, but some were abandoned headstones from Mountain View Cemetery. "Wherever we could get stone, especially granite, we would send out our trucks and machinery and pick them up," he said.

Long after Cunningham hung up his trowel in 1955, he'd head down to supervise the crew that continued work on the seawall. He died in 1963 and never saw it completed. But according to his granddaughter Julia, he never really left. She says Stuart Lefeaux arranged to have the ashes of Jimmy and his wife, Elizabeth—they died within months of each other—buried behind the plaque in his honour at Siwash Rock.

He's remembered through the annual James Cunningham Seawall Race, which started in 1971—the year the last stone was laid on the seawall.

James "Jimmy" Cunningham, stonemason, was the craftsman behind the beautiful seawall around Stanley Park. In this 1962 photo he is seen working his way south from Siwash Rock. And despite the wall, an afternoon stroll can still be a wet adventure for the unwary.
Province, *Gordon Sedawie photo*

THE PIONEER CEMETERY

Local historian Maurice Guibord estimates there are up to 200 bodies buried along the stretch of Stanley Park that runs from Brockton Point Lighthouse to the Nine O'Clock Gun.

Courtesy Maurice Guibord, 2020

Mountain View Cemetery may have been Vancouver's first official cemetery when it opened in 1886, but it certainly wasn't the first. Bodies had been buried on Deadman's Island in Coal Harbour for thousands of years, and those who didn't want their relatives interred alongside the socially undesirable, the diseased or the unchristened moved their burials farther into Stanley Park. "Its very association with the First Nations and Chinese immigrants thus designated Deadman's Island as a resting place for the pagan, the unchristened, and the socially and culturally anathematized," says local historian Maurice Guibord.

The stretch of land from Brockton Point Lighthouse to the Nine O'Clock Gun had always been a burial ground for the Indigenous people who lived there, but as Gastown was settled, it also became an alternative burial ground known as the Pioneer Cemetery.

Chinese people were initially buried there, but for most, it was only temporary. The custom was to return the bones to China eventually, so the graves were shallow to allow for faster decomposition and easier exhumation. Once the body had turned to bones, they were dug up by bone collectors, cleaned, packaged and returned to China. Failure to do this was said to create *po*—homeless and malevolent ghosts who stuck around and haunted living relatives.

Maurice has found evidence that there are up to 200 bodies still buried along the peninsula, including the remains of settlers, some Chinese people and the Indigenous people who had abandoned the custom of above-ground burials.

The graves weren't officially marked and the burials weren't recorded, so when the perimeter road was built around Stanley Park in the late 1880s, the bodies were simply paved over. "They are buried under the road, under the trees, under the bike path and the walkway. They are all through there," says Maurice. Something to think about the next time you're sitting in the parking lot or taking a walk along the seawall.

THE LAST SQUATTER

Even before Tim Cummings' body was cold, the parks board was getting ready to tear down his home of seventy-seven years. Tim was born in a cottage near Brockton Point in 1881. He was the son of James Cummings, a Scot, and Lucy, a Nuxalk woman from Bella Coola. The Cummings settled in a little green house on just over half an acre (.2 hectares), surrounded by fruit trees, boysenberries and lilac bushes. It had a large white flagpole in the front and was a landmark in the park, later known just as Tim's Place. Their neighbours were mostly the families of Portuguese sailors who had jumped ship and married Squamish women.

A small number of squatters continued to live in Stanley Park into the twentieth century but lost a series of legal cases during the squatter eviction trials. Only "Aunt Sally" Kulkalem, from the Squamish band, was able to prove that she had occu-pied her land at Lumberman's Arch for the required sixty years of continued tenancy.

Those squatters who stayed were turned into tenants, paying the parks board one dollar a month, which eventually increased to five dollars, until only siblings Agnes and Tim Cummings were left. They kept their cottage lit with porcelain coal oil lamps.

Tim was the oldest of five children and the last to survive. He died in 1958.

The *Vancouver Sun* kicked in with an editorial appeal to the city to save the cottage and turn it into a museum. Major J.S. Matthews, who had interviewed Tim and Agnes in 1939, was intent on saving the house: "I believe the board is called the board of parks and public recreation. It should be called the board of parks and public desecration," the archivist told a reporter.[16]

The *Vancouver Sun*'s editors called for a civic historic sites and monuments board in an editorial that described a reality eerily similar to today's: "Every day in this city, houses and buildings are disappearing."[17]

The parks board backed down and voted to spend $2,000 to renovate and preserve the house as a historic site. Instead, they moved it to another section of the park and waited for it to deteriorate. Five years later, Alderman George Puil described the house as hideous and said it should be demolished, claiming that "many people have threatened to push the cottage into the harbour." He got his way with a 5–1 vote, and Tim's place was gone.[18]

Tim Cummings at home in Stanley Park, October 5, 1953.
Vancouver Archives St Pk P249.2

WEST OF MAIN STREET

GHOST SIGNS

There are ghost signs all over Vancouver. Sometimes we embrace them and they become a fixture on a building, but mostly, they are uncovered by construction workers one day and covered again the next.

Chinatown ghost sign for Wild Rose Cake and Pastry Flour.
Fritz Autzen photo, 1960

In October 2018, Fatidjah Nestman was looking out her high-rise window on West Thirteenth Avenue and noticed an old painted ad for White's Grocery had popped up when workers removed the cement siding from a building on Granville Street.

"I wonder how old this is," Fatidjah said to me. "The phone number Bay 433 predates the sixties." It certainly did. White's Grocery was at 2932 Granville from 1915 until 1931. It was owned by Thomas and Mary White, who lived nearby, on Thirteenth Avenue.

In 2018, the ground floor retail at 2932 Granville included a shoe store, a women's clothing boutique and a lingerie shop. The four apartments above with the big bay windows looked empty.

Ghost signs are a pre-billboard form of advertising that date back to the 1890s, though most of the ones that have appeared in Vancouver seem to be from the 1920s and '30s. Some of the surviving signs include the advertising on the old Woodward's Building, Rennie's Seeds in False Creek, Shelly's Bakery on Victoria Drive,

Money's Mushrooms on Prior Street, Wild Rose Flour in Chinatown and Royal Crown Soap on the London Hotel at East Georgia and Main Street.

The day after Fatidjah sent me the photo of the White's Grocery ghost sign, she told me, "Good thing we got the photo yesterday; today they are nailing siding over it. It was a dream, now it's gone. I wonder if the workers took any photos?"

I highly doubt it. But I guess that's why they're called ghost signs, because of their ephemeral existence.

2932 Granville Street, October 2018.
Karen Fiorini photo

PERCY LINDEN'S HOUSE

In 2005, Heritage Vancouver released its annual list of endangered properties. High on that list were the residential houses of the Downtown South area, a former working-class neighbourhood that developed between 1890 and 1910 and was once dotted with small warehouses, offices, autobody shops, nightclubs, a few apartment buildings, parking lots and houses. Heritage Vancouver was right. Later that year, 909 Richards Street, an 1889 house and one of the oldest in the area, met the bulldozer. As of 2020, there were just thirteen houses remaining in the entire Downtown South neighbourhood.

Percy Linden was one of the last holdouts of the Richards Street homeowners. He lived at number 1021, between Nelson and Helmcken Streets. A truck driver for most of his life, Linden bought the house in the 1950s and, soon afterwards, left to work in the oil fields of Alberta. He rented the house out and didn't move back until 1970.

In 1993, Linden won an award for his garden from the BC Society of Landscape Architects. "I never, ever thought of what I do in terms of landscaping," Linden told a reporter. "I didn't have the faintest intention of even growing a weed. I just set out to clean up the yard, and it evolved, inch by inch. People talk about hours of planning. I didn't put one second's planning into it; I just dug wherever I felt like it."[1] A little sign in the front yard read: "Take a little extra time today to stop and smell the roses along the way."

Linden didn't have a special affinity for birds, either, but he built birdcages, dozens of them. Some were colonial style, some Swiss. There were farmhouses, barns,

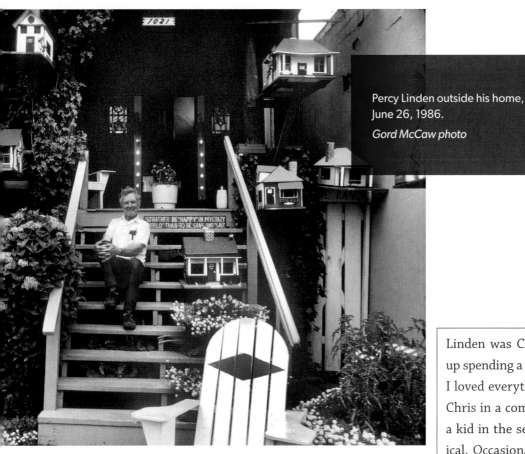

Percy Linden outside his home, June 26, 1986.
Gord McCaw photo

hotels and windmills he said were inspired by his rural Alberta upbringing.

He was there when a car dealership popped up across the road. And still there when David Y.H. Lui leased the buildings on that stretch of Richards and turned number 1036 into a theatre. He may even have caught a glimpse of some of the actors from a slew of musical revues, comedies and children's stories, and he was there in 1980 when the theatre changed to a rock and roll club called the Laundromat, which shortly after became Richard's on Richards.

Linden was Chris Cound's uncle. "I grew up spending a lot of time in that house and I loved everything about that place," says Chris in a comment on my blog. "Even as a kid in the seventies I knew it was magical. Occasionally, I helped paint the odd birdhouse that would hang out front for the upcoming spring season. I still have the sign he painted for me that says: 'I'd rather be happy in my crazy world than to be sane and sad.'"

Tour buses stopped outside Linden's house, tourists snapped photographs and others left fan mail in his mailbox. But every year, the house would seem to shrink a little more as a sea of high-rises and condominiums grew up around it. In July 2009, Richard's on Richards hosted its last gig. By then, Linden and his little house had already left the block.

THE OTHER HOUSES OF DOWNTOWN SOUTH

One of Percy Linden's neighbours on Richards Street was a feisty little old lady named Linda Rupa, who bought her small green cottage and the lot next door in 1962. Rupa had knocked back an offer to buy her out for $3 million, but by 2007, she was struggling under the weight of a $36,000 annual property tax bill. She was also looking at the destruction of her neighbourhood, as all around her, houses—many still in good shape—were being replaced by condo towers.

During the 1940s and '50s, Rupa's house had been a speakeasy for a bootlegger.

"When I came in here, I had 17 phones, two private lines to the States and a big poker table upstairs," she told *Vancouver Sun* reporter John Mackie in 2007. "It was a lovely neighbourhood, where people cared about each other."

Rupa, a former Safeway cashier, sold the house to the Aquilini Group, who also owned the Richard's on Richards site, as well as the Vancouver Canucks, for $6 million. She told Mackie she was looking for a small house with a little garden, maybe in New Westminster. To celebrate, she told him, she bought a nice tube of lipstick, and she'd be buying a quilt from Sears on sale. "Do you remember the house with the birdhouses outside? That was Percy Linden," she told Mackie. "He lived here as long as I did. He sold his house and three months later he had passed away. He was a lovely fellow."[2]

It was too late for Linden's house, but five of the houses built between 1907 and 1909 were saved, including Rupa's little cottage—now number 477 Helmcken. Three of the houses are on their original lot, and two were moved from Richards Street—the other one at 1080 Richards is now 487 Helmcken.

431–439 Helmcken Street serves as a reminder of what was once a thriving working-class neighbourhood. *Eve Lazarus photo, 2020*

IACI'S CASA CAPRI

Eva and Frank Iaci.
Courtesy Maria and Rick Iaci

In 2004, shortly after 1022 Seymour Street sold, Rick Iaci pulled his car into the back lane. The house had been his family's restaurant for more than fifty years, and he was horrified to see dozens of framed autographed photographs and other memorabilia piled up outside ready to be thrown into a Dumpster. "Take it all," his cousin Teenie told him. "As you can see it's all going into the Dumpster." So Rick did, and in that moment, saved a piece of Vancouver's history.

Frank and Eva Iaci were cousins to the Filippones who ran the Penthouse Nightclub across the street and lived in the house next door to it at number 1033 that Giuseppe and Maria Filippone had bought in 1932. The house and the strip club are still there, run by Danny Filippone, the founder's nephew. The Iaci's famous house, unfortunately, is not.

The Iaci's raised their six children in number 1022, turning it into a bootlegging joint during the Depression. Eva started making plates of pasta so that her customers could have something to eat while they drank. The menu was simple: spaghetti with meatballs, T-bone steak, ravioli, chicken cacciatore. Her food proved really popular and soon the house became known as Casa Capri.

Iaci's is on the far left in this 1981 photo of the 1000 block of Seymour Street.
Vancouver Archives 779-E06.35

The family called it number 1022; locals just called it Iaci's.

Iaci's was gone by the time I arrived in Vancouver; it closed in 1982. I first heard about it when I was researching my true crime book *Murder by Milkshake*. Before Rene Castellani murdered his wife, Esther, the family would spend a few nights a week in the restaurant, helping out in the kitchen or just hanging out. "We were at Iaci's all the time. I don't even know how many times a week," says the Castellanis' daughter, Jeannine. "We never sat in the restaurant. We were always in the kitchen where they were cooking." When it got late, Jeannine was put to bed in Eva's downstairs suite, which also harboured the illegal booze. "When the police came in, they never checked because they saw me there, sound asleep," she says.

Customers could park for free in the tiny lot in the back, go through the basement, climb up the stairs to the back porch and then enter through the kitchen. Someone would be there to greet them, take their coats and find them a seat in one of the three small front rooms, where they could check out the Iacis' old wedding photos or framed covers of *Life* and *Look* magazines.

Rick Iaci remembers a time when the bathroom walls were covered in stock certificates. One night a broker was using the facilities when he noticed that one of the old stocks was worth money. "They took down half the wall to get it," says Rick. The magazine covers went up after that.

Casa Capri was the place to go for anyone looking for a good meal and a drink late at night. After performing at the Palomar or

the Cave, stars such as Dean Martin, Red Skelton, Tom Jones, Louis Armstrong, and Sonny and Cher would head to Iaci's with an autographed photo made out to one of the family members—usually one of Eva's daughters, Koko, Teenie and Toots. Rick is now the guardian of the old photos. He spent every Saturday night for more than ten years at Casa Capri, sometimes as the bartender when the regular guy didn't turn up. Once he asked Eva why they were mixing Tang with the vodka instead of orange juice. She told him: "If it's good enough for the astronauts, it's good enough for our customers."

In 2005, Eva and Frank Iaci were posthumously inducted into the BC Restaurant Hall of Fame.

TOP Maria, Rick, Jeannine and her daughter, Ashley, at the book launch for *Murder by Milkshake*, November 2018.

Scott Alexander photo

BOTTOM One of the autographed posters saved from the Dumpster by Rick Iaci. Big Fannie Annie was a regular after-hours customer at Casa Capri when she performed at the Penthouse Nightclub in 1979 and 1980.

Maria and Rick Iaci collection

THE CAMBIE STREET ROCKET SHIP

Have you ever wondered why there's a snazzy-looking rocket ship at the southwest end of the Cambie Street Bridge? It was built for Expo 86, then relocated by helicopter to its current site after the fair ended. It's actually a replica of a rocket ship that was designed by Lew Parry and built by Neon Products for the Sheet Metal Workers Local 280 as a float in the 1936 Pacific National Exhibition parade to celebrate Vancouver's fiftieth birthday. The original streamlined rocket ship sat at the Vancouver Airport terminal until 1972, when its rusting frame was thrown into the landfill. The replica was made using old photos of the original and advice from Parry, who turned eighty as Vancouver celebrated its centennial. This replica is made of hardier stuff than its predecessor—stainless steel and brass, which will hopefully see it through another 100 years.

TOP The original rocket ship at Vancouver Airport, 1947.
Vancouver Archives 1376-360

BOTTOM The rocket ship has lived at the south end of the Cambie Street Bridge since 1986.
Eve Lazarus photo, 2020

Inspector Ian MacGregor carries the axe from the crime scene on East 22nd Street.

Vancouver Sun, *December 10, 1965*

MOUNT PLEASANT AXE MURDER

When police arrived at the house at Main Street and East Twenty-second Avenue early in the morning of December 9, 1965, the first thing they saw was the bright red Santa Claus painted on the front window. When they kicked in the front door, the horrified officers found the bloodied bodies of Osborne Kosberg, thirty-nine, his wife, Dorothy, forty, and four of their six children. Barry, fifteen, died in his bedroom at the back of the house. Gayle, eleven, was dead in the bedroom she shared with her sister. Two-year-old Vincent died from deep wounds to the face and skull. Marianne, thirteen, died in the hospital nine days later. The family members had been slaughtered with a double-bladed axe. Only the baby, the Kosberg's sixth and youngest child survived.

The older children attended nearby Sir Charles Tupper Secondary School. Thomas, the oldest child at seventeen, had a history of mental illness, but no one could imagine him plotting a murder, let alone killing his own family. On the night of the murder, Thomas bought a bottle of twenty-five sleeping pills from a local drugstore. He made chocolate milkshakes for his mother, for Florence, a family friend who was visiting, and for his two brothers and two sisters. The family was watching television. Florence

Osborne and Dorothy Kosberg and four of their children: Marianne, thirteen; Barry, fifteen; Thomas, seventeen; front row, Gayle, eleven.

Vancouver Sun, *December 10, 1965*

sat at one end of the chesterfield while Thomas sat at the other, reading a book. She remembers Dorothy saying, "I didn't know that I was that tired." Florence then fell asleep and woke up about eleven p.m. Thomas suggested she stay the night, but she called a taxi and left. While the rest of his family slept, Thomas waited up for Osborne, who was working a late shift as a truck driver for Allied Heat and Fuel.

When Osborne came home, Thomas made his dad a milkshake.

At four a.m., when everyone was asleep, Thomas went to the basement to fetch the axe. After hacking up his family, Thomas changed his clothes and drove off in the family's 1954 sedan and crashed it into a power pole. He then stole a car, drove back to within a block of his home and phoned Robert Estergaard, a counsellor at Central

City Mission who kept a house for disturbed boys and where Thomas had lived for six months before being sent to Crease Clinic of Psychological Medicine at Riverview Hospital in Coquitlam. Estergaard then drove to the Kosberg's house and found Thomas sitting on the front porch. He didn't go inside, didn't know what Thomas had done, and drove the boy to the house of Dr Bennet Wong, Thomas's psychologist at the Crease Clinic. Dr Wong called the police, who when they arrived at his West Vancouver home, found Thomas "neatly dressed" and "calm."[3]

> At Thomas's February 1967 trial, two psychiatrists told the court that he was a schizophrenic, quite capable of carrying out a "complex and deliberate plan" but incapable of distinguishing whether what he was doing was right or wrong. The court ruled Thomas not guilty of six counts of capital murder by reason of insanity and shipped him back to Riverview Hospital.

Thomas was released from Riverview in September 1977. Dr John Duffy, director of the Forensic Psychiatric Services Commission, said that Thomas was "a sober, sensible fellow" who furthered his education while in custody. "I haven't any doubt at all that he's a model citizen and that's the last we'll ever hear about him."[4] Duffy said that children who kill their parents do so almost always because of some problem in their family history, and never murder again. Thomas worked as a biomedical engineer at BC Children's Hospital for the next thirty years. He married Maggie, who had five children from a previous relationship. His stepchildren only discovered his story after he died in 2016.

The post on my blog about the Kosberg murders is one of the most visited of all my stories. It has also elicited dozens of comments. Some of the most interesting are from Maggie's family and people who knew Tom and wanted to stay anonymous.

"I met Tom in his last few years at Riverview. He was an amazingly intelligent man, with a good heart, but a tortured soul," wrote one. "We were close friends for the next few years after his release. I'm glad he found true happiness with Maggie. Tom will

The Kosberg house at 142 East Twenty-second Street in 2020.

Eve Lazarus photo

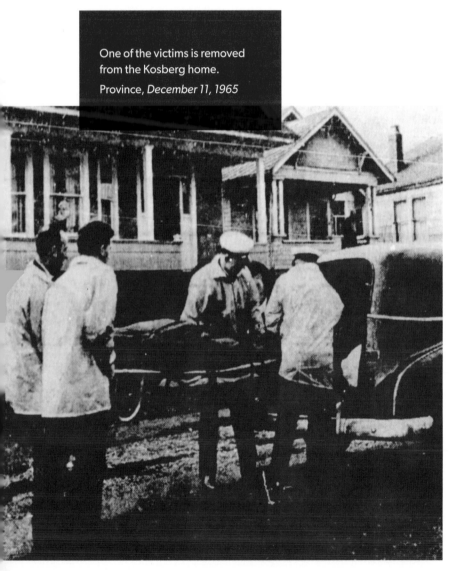

One of the victims is removed from the Kosberg home.
Province, *December 11, 1965*

be remembered always as a kind, loving, intelligent and giving person."

I received this email from a woman who was married to Maggie's son: "My family were very close with Tom for many years and up until his death. We had absolutely no idea about his past until three days after his passing," she wrote. "To us, he was family—a very caring and kind man with a twinkle in his eye and a wonderful sense of humour. It's taken me over a year to process the discovery of this shocking information and to be able to separate his tragic past from the man that I loved as a second father. I found it a little odd that he never spoke of his family over all the years that I knew him but I thought that they must not have been close and never pressed the issue."

Two decades after the murders, tragedy still dogged the family. Thomas' uncle, Arthur Riggs, who had signed the death certificate for his sister Dorothy and his nieces and nephews, killed himself in 1987 by jumping out of the tenth-floor window of Vancouver General Hospital.

KING EDWARD HIGH SCHOOL

On June 19, 1973, a three-alarm fire broke out at Vancouver City College at West Twelfth Avenue and Oak Street. More than 1,000 students were attending classes and safely evacuated, but it was too late for the school. The building was destroyed by faulty wiring in the attic.

William T. Whiteway, the same architect who designed the Sun Tower, designed the school in the neoclassical style and topped it off with a central cupola. It was the first secondary school in Vancouver to be built south of False Creek, and was appropriately named Vancouver High School. Classes started in 1890, the school was renamed King Edward High School in 1910 and another section was added two years later.

The list of King Ed alumni includes an impressive array of Vancouver luminaries, such as the philanthropist Cecil Green and broadcasters Jack Cullen and Red Robinson. Other notables to pass through the school's corridors are Dal Grauer, president and chair of BC Power Corporation and BC Electric; Nathan Nemetz, Chief Justice of the Supreme Court of BC; Grace McCarthy, politician; Yvonne De Carlo, actor; Jack Wasserman, newspaper reporter; educator Dr Annie B. Jamieson; and Olympic athlete Percy Williams.

In 1962, King Ed became an adult education centre and the kids were transferred to Eric Hamber Secondary, says Andrea Nicholson, alumni coordinator. Vancouver City College took over the King Ed building in 1965. Blog commenter David Byrnes attended first-year university there in the late 1960s. "One day when we were goofing around my friend Malcolm told me he'd found a way into the attic," says David. "I remember climbing up to look out the cupola and finding a rifle range."

Andrea confirms that there was a rifle range, and students from Cecil Rhodes and Henry Hudson elementary schools used to train there. Andrea's mother, Elizabeth (Maclaine) Lowe, taught at the school and later became department head for business education. She was supposed to teach night school on the day the school burned down. "I remember as a child going up into the turret, and I remember when they pulled that school apart the dividers for the bathroom stalls were solid marble," says Andrea, who could see the flames from the grounds of Cecil Rhodes Elementary at West Fourteenth Avenue and Spruce.

Vancouver General Hospital bought the King Edward building and land in 1970, though it remained an educational institution until the mid-1980s. Now, all that's left is the stone wall at Oak and West Twelfth Avenue, a stained-glass window installed in Vancouver Community College's Broadway campus, and, in the Gordon and Leslie Diamond Health Care Centre that replaced the school, there is a plaque, a large photograph of the original school and a circle of yellow tile in the lobby outlining the original King Edward High School.

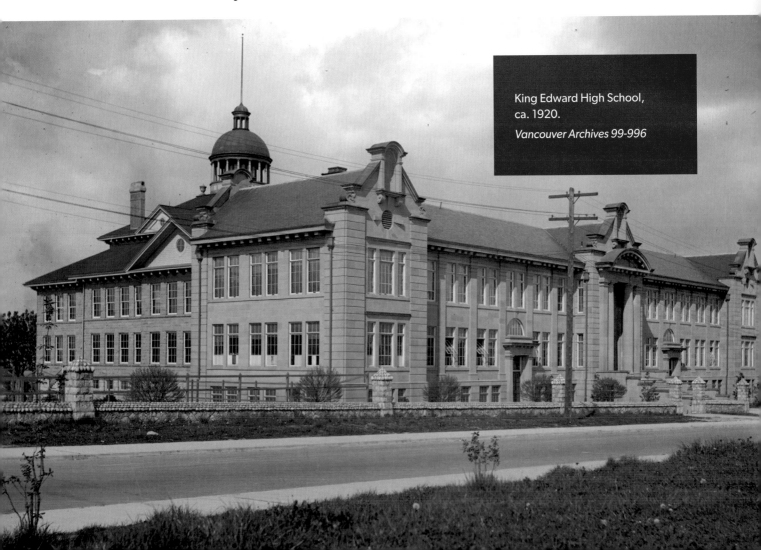

King Edward High School, ca. 1920.
Vancouver Archives 99-996

Percy Williams outside his Mount Pleasant house in 1928, the year he competed in the Amsterdam Summer Olympic Games.

Vancouver Archives 99-3638

WHEN HARRY MET PERCY

There's a young, very thin Percy Williams in a picture of the King Edward High School track team of 1926. Williams had taken up running two years earlier, when his gym teacher noticed how much faster he was than the other boys his age and bullied him into joining the track team. Two years later, he brought home two gold medals from the Olympics and became a local hero.

Percy Williams died on November 29, 1982. I reckon his life and his death is worth writing about, because in these days of super-charged Olympic athletes, Williams was truly unique.

Williams was born in 1908 and spent a good chunk of his life on West Twelfth Avenue in Mount Pleasant. He was a scrawny kid, standing just five foot six (1.7 metres) and weighing 110 pounds (fifty kilograms), with a bad heart from childhood rheumatic fever. He was eighteen when he was "discovered" while attending King Edward High School.

His coach, Bob Granger, told a reporter that he took Williams on after he tied a race with his sprint champion in 1926. "It violated every known principle of the running game," he said. "He ran with his arms glued to his sides. It actually made me tired to watch him."[5] Granger had interesting training techniques. His idea of a warm-up was having Williams lie on the dressing table under a pile of blankets. Another was making him run flat out into a mattress propped up against a wall. Unorthodox maybe, but Williams kept winning.

By 1928, Williams had bulked up to 125 pounds (55 kilograms). That was the year he brought home two gold medals for the 200-metre and 100-metre sprints at the Amsterdam Olympics. The newspapers dubbed him "Peerless Percy," and he returned to Vancouver to a hero's welcome from 40,000 people. Kids got the day off school, and a candy manufacturer brought out an "Our Percy" chocolate bar.

Williams was a reluctant star, and when a leg injury ended his track career in 1932, he seemed relieved. He told a reporter: "Oh, I was so glad to get out of it all."[6] By 1935, the public had forgotten all about him, and he quietly soldiered on as an insurance salesman.

Williams held on to his record for the 200-metre dash for three decades—until another Vancouverite, Harry Jerome, set a new mark. On May 30, 1959, Harry Jerome met Percy Williams—the two most remarkable sprinters in Vancouver's history. Tragically, both men died in 1982. Jerome died at forty-two from a brain aneurysm just eight days after Williams, suffering from arthritis, shot himself in the head while in the bath in his West End home. He was seventy-four.

Harry Jerome meets Percy Williams after breaking the older man's record set three decades earlier.

Province, *Bill Cunningham photo, May 30, 1959*

THE MAHARAJA OF ALLEEBABA

A few months after my book *Murder by Milkshake* came out in 2018, Bob Shiell sent me a note from Calgary. He told me that he had worked with Rene Castellani at CKNW and played a big role in one of the radio station's most audacious promotions—the Maharaja of Alleebaba.

This was the early 1960s, a time when no promotion was considered too outrageous or too racist in the continuous quest for ratings, and Bob's insights and photos were a great addition to the information that I had included in my book.

Bob told me that in 1963, he was twenty-two and worked in the promotions department of CKNW. Rival station CKLG had brought to town Marvin Miller, star of an American TV program called *The Millionaire* in which Miller gave away money to people he'd never met. CKLG saw this as a great way to get a boost in

the upcoming ratings war and had Miller go around the city handing out cash. "We had to come up with an idea for something that would counter that," says Bob—and the Maharaja was born. "The idea was that he was coming over to buy the province of British Columbia."

Charismatic radio host Rene Castellani was hired to dress up as the Maharaja. Bob played Ugie, his driver, and wore a red tunic and striped pants. "We had a crossed sword logo made with sticky tape and we put that on the passenger and the driver's door, and I found a little flag— the kind of embassy flag that you see on the president's car. It was actually the flag of the Republic of Germany, but nobody noticed," says Bob. The black Rolls-Royce was a loaner from one of the station's owners—Robert Ballard, of the Dr. Ballard's dog food company. They hired

an off-duty motorcycle cop to provide an escort and two women who normally did supermarket demonstrations to dress up as harem girls.

They stashed the Rolls at Bob's mother's house on Granville Street, met there each morning and put on their costumes in the basement. For two weeks the entourage drove around Vancouver—to clubs, restaurants, hotels, drive-ins and even a BC Lions game at Empire Stadium—often accompanied by a CKNW reporter named Sherwin Shragge (yes, that's his real name) who would interview them on the radio. "I had this big leather suitcase handcuffed to my wrist full of silver dollars," says Bob.

Rene, says Bob, was born for the role. "He loved the attention, he loved the harem girls, he loved riding around in the Rolls-Royce. It was the ideal role for him." In fact, it was so successful that outraged locals came out with their handmade signs that said, "Keep BC British."

"A lot of people took it really seriously," says Bob. "They really bought into this whole idea. CKNW did a really good job of selling this concept of a guy coming in to buy the province."

TOP The Maharaja of Alleebaba was a CKNW promotion in 1963.
Courtesy Bob Shiell

BOTTOM Rene Castellani as the Maharaja of Alleebaba and Bob Shiell as his driver, 1963.
Courtesy Bob Shiell

BC FERRIES AND THE RUSSIAN FREIGHTER

One of the highlights of taking a ferry from Vancouver to Victoria is traversing Active Pass, that narrow channel of water that runs through the Gulf Islands. It's particularly interesting when two ferries are travelling in different directions at the same time, forcing them to hug opposing shores. It's also the riskiest part of the crossing for ferry captains.

Captain James Pollock was in charge of the *Queen of Victoria* and its 500-plus passengers on August 2, 1970. It was a clear morning and the waters were calm when he entered Active Pass. Although Pollock wouldn't have been expecting to see the *Sergey Yesenin*, a 14,700-ton Russian freighter bound for Vancouver with a full load of steel and cars, in those days it wasn't unusual for deep-sea freighters to take a shortcut through Active Pass, cutting off nine miles (fourteen kilometres) from their trip.

Captain Pollock made a radio call announcing his entry into the channel, but the ferry and the ship ran on different radio frequencies and no one answered him.

David G. Crabbe was the Canadian pilot aboard the *Sergey Yesenin* that day. The Russian captain, Nikolai Khauston, was unfamiliar with BC waters, and it was Crabbe's job to get the freighter safely to Vancouver. Crabbe was unaware that the *Queen of Victoria* was running late out of Tsawwassen, and he took the freighter through the shorter route. Instead of taking a long turn, the freighter made a sharp entry, which turned into a wide swing into mid-channel as it moved through the Pass. The two vessels collided and, stuck together by the impact of the crash, slowly pinwheeled through the J-shaped channel.

Ray Williams was fishing in Active Pass that day and captured the impact and aftermath on his movie camera. He filmed the freighter's steel bow slicing through the ferry's portside, almost cutting it in half. Before it stopped, it had knifed through two levels of outside deck and penetrated almost to the middle of the forward lounge in the passenger deck. The steel ceiling was crushed to the floor, and chairs, where passengers had been sitting, were obliterated. Glass and magazines littered the floor. A broken pipe poured water onto the carpet.

Scott Watson's father, Edwin, was aboard the ferry that day. "My dad saw the freighter coming. He stood up and shouted for passengers to move to the far side of the lounge area. When they just stared at him, he began physically shoving them out of the way," says Scott. "He got a letter of appreciation from the BC Ferry Corporation."

Eight people were injured. Annie Hammond, a thirty-year-old schoolteacher from Victoria, and her seven-month-old baby, Peter, as well as seventeen-year-old Sheila Mae Taylor from New Jersey, were killed.

Phylis Everlie Songhurst wasn't on the ferry that day, but the event is firmly seared into her memory. "This was three days before my twelfth birthday," she said. "I was in the Resthaven Hospital having my appendix removed. Annie Hammond died in the bed next to me."

The Russian freighter came out of the accident with two holes in the prow and some scratches to the paint. The investigation initially blamed both BC Ferries Captain James Pollock and David Crabbe, the pilot aboard the *Sergey Yesenin*. But in the end, the bulk of the blame was placed on the Russian freighter. Pollock was reinstated two months later and Crabbe was cleared on appeal. The Russians paid BC Ferries $550,000 in damages, the costs of damages to their own ship, as well as sixty percent of all third-party claims.[7]

The *Queen of Victoria* was repaired and put back into service. An upper deck was added in 1981, and it was part of the fleet until 2000, when BC Ferries sold the vessel to a company based in the Dominican Republic.

The Russian freighter *Sergey Yesenin* smashes into the *Queen of Victoria* ferry in Active Pass, killing three people, the first fatalities in a BC Ferries accident.

Vancouver Sun, *Brian Kent photo, August 2, 1970*

HOW THE MUSEUM OF EXOTIC WORLD BECAME NEPTOON RECORDS

Neptoon Records at 3561 Main Street.

Eve Lazarus photo, 2018

Guessing the number of albums in Neptoon Records is a bit like guessing the number of jelly beans in a jar. There are thousands and thousands of them. You can find them filed neatly in the store, stacked down the stairs and filling the basement. Founder and owner Rob Frith tells me that he had to stop renting out one of the upstairs rooms so that he could use it for storage.

"People who collect are obsessive," says Rob. He knows because he's a collector—records, posters, menus, old contracts, buttons, photographs and concert ticket stubs.

If record shops are a dying breed, you sure wouldn't know it at Neptoon. The place is packed with browsers, and most of them are young. You can pick up a used album for as little as a dollar or pay up to $1,500 for a 1960s sealed copy of a record by a Canadian band called the Haunted. Most will set you back between five and twenty-five dollars.

In 1980, Rob was working in construction. Then the economy crashed, and he started casting around for things to do. He knew two things: he didn't want to work for anyone, and he liked collecting vinyl. "One day, I thought maybe I should open a record store." His first store opened on Fraser Street in January 1981.

After a few years the area started to go downhill and Rob needed more space. "I was driving down Main Street one day and saw a 'for sale' sign on a building. I called the realtor and the building was way cheaper than I thought it would be. I bought it for $365,000. It had two rental suites upstairs so it worked out great as far as my overhead."

His store is now the oldest independent record store in Vancouver. It's survived CDs and iTunes and Spotify. "We hung on long enough that there was a resurgence almost twenty years ago," says Rob. "It's gone leaps and bounds since then."

The renewed interest in vinyl started when kids wanted to be deejays, and increased when they found Mum and Dad's turntable and old records in the basement. Now, music labels are releasing new pressings and reissues creating a whole new market for vinyl.

Rob, it turns out, wasn't the only owner of this building who liked collecting.

The storefront first pops up in the city directories in 1951, owned by Harold and Barbara Morgan. The Morgans lived upstairs and ran a spray-paint rental business downstairs. Every year the couple travelled to a different place—New Guinea, Borneo, Africa, Guatemala—and brought back souvenirs. When they retired in 1989, they turned the store into the (free) Museum of Exotic World and packed it full of collectibles such as a stuffed alligator, butterflies, a shrunken head and hundreds of photographs. They opened the store for a few hours each day. When the Morgans died they bequeathed their vast collection, and their ashes, to Alexander Lamb's antique store just down the road. In 2020, a display was still there on the back wall.

TOP Nardwuar and Rob Frith at Neptoon Records.

Dale Shippam photo, Nardwuar.com

BOTTOM The remains of the Museum of Exotic World.

Tom Carter photo, 2020

MAIN STREET FARMERS' MARKET

More than 3,000 people came out for the opening of City Market on August 15, 1908.

Neil Whaley collection

False Creek is a realtor's dream. It's a model of sustainability, with housing options—that include the condos and townhouses in the Olympic Village—a school, a seawall for walking and running and biking, and a waterway filled on any given day with kayaks and canoes and dragon boats. The neighbourhood has fitness facilities, outdoor play areas, breweries and artistic venues—even a science centre left over from the heyday of Expo 86. And, if you still have to leave its borders, downtown is just a short jog away.

But in 1908, when Vancouver got its first farmers' market, False Creek was a strange choice of location, with an abattoir for a neighbour and a streetcar ride from the city centre. False Creek covered about five times the area it does today, and City Market was accessible only by bridge. It was situated at the southwest intersection bordered by Main Street, Quebec Street and Terminal Avenue—rather ironically, where the McDonald's parking lot is today.

City Market was an elaborate building, set on pilings, designed by William T. Whiteway. It had twin bell towers and large arched windows, and looked like an exhibition hall.

Unfortunately, the market itself was a financial failure and limped along until it burned down in a spectacular and mysterious fire that originated from Pearson Iron Works at 3:30 a.m. on November 10, 1925.

THE ROYAL HUDSON GOES SOUTH

On March 20, 1977, hundreds of people lined the Arbutus Street corridor to get a look at the Royal Hudson locomotive No. 2860 as it passed, chugging its way from the old BC Hydro yards in Kitsilano to Marpole, then to New Westminster, through White Rock and across the US border into Blaine, Washington. It was part of a three-week promotional tour spearheaded by travel minister Grace McCarthy and Vancouver mayor Jack Volrich. The steam engine hauled seven cars filled with BC artifacts, including a variety of models, maps and posters of BC's resource-based industries. Because it was Queen Elizabeth's silver jubilee, one of the cars had been turned into a royal suite, complete with life-sized waxworks of Her Majesty, Prince Philip and Prince Charles.

"I heard a steam whistle and I knew that something was going along the Kitsilano trestle. I could see smoke coming up from that area, so I got into my car and drove recklessly across Broadway, parked near Arbutus, got out of my car and took a grab shot. There was no time to set up," says photographer Angus McIntyre. When Angus had a show of his photographs at the Baron Gallery in 2012, legendary street photographer Fred Herzog attended. He bought a copy of Angus's photo of the Royal Hudson, and told him that some of his best photos were grab shots.

For twenty-five years, the No. 2860, built in Montreal in 1940, had a regular run from North Vancouver to Squamish. That ended in 1999, when the engine's boiler gave out. Aside from a couple of appearances over the years where the engine was taken out for a ride in public, it has been on display at the West Coast Railway Heritage Park in Squamish. The Arbutus corridor is now a fancy bike and pedestrian trail. Abe van Oeveren tells me that the last train to run on the line was on May 31, 2001. "CPR 1237, affectionately known as 'Queenie,' lifted the last two empty malt hoppers from the Molson's brewery by the Burrard Bridge."

The Royal Hudson travelling along the Arbutus corridor at Broadway.

Angus McIntyre photo, 1977

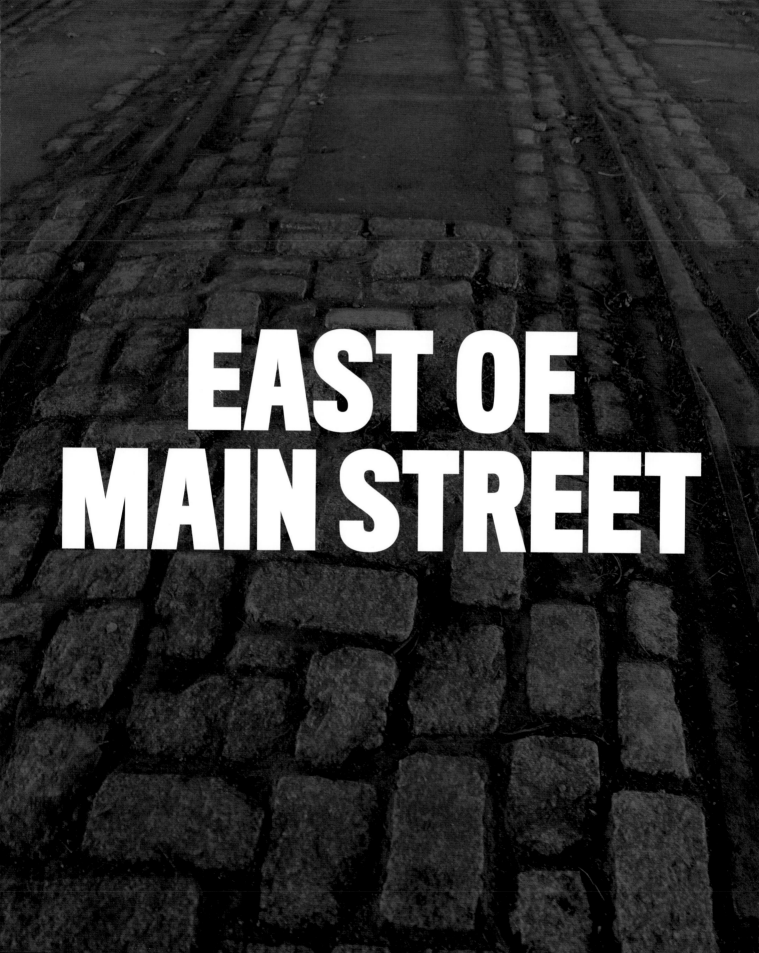

A BRIDGE, A TUNNEL AND A FAKE HOUSE

There is a fake house at the corner of Frances Street and Ingleton Avenue in the residential suburb of Burnaby that has fooled even some of its closest neighbours since 1967. Rumours have spread that it's everything from a government safe house to an animal crematorium, but the truth is far more interesting.

The house, set next to a nicely landscaped garden, is actually a huge ventilation shaft that's hidden in plain sight and sits about 150 feet (forty-five metres) above the CN tracks at the midpoint of the Thornton Tunnel. Instead of a kitchen and dining room, ventilation machines and very big fans operate inside. The tip-off is the metal "keep out" wrought-iron fence, the absence of windows and the concrete barriers where a front porch would typically be.

The Thornton Tunnel took CN two years to build and opened in 1968. It's 2.1 miles (3.4 kilometres) long and runs from the south end of the Ironworkers Memorial Bridge, under Burnaby and comes out at Dawson Street behind some warehouses.

Larry Lundgren was a switchman for CN from 1967 to 1972 and frequently found himself stuck at the wrong end of the train after a ten-to-fifteen-minute ride through the tunnel. "As sure

South portal of the Thornton Tunnel.
Angus McIntyre photo, 1975

BOTTOM LEFT CN's fake Burnaby house.
Eve Lazarus photo, 2020

as heck a ship would come along and the bridge span would be lifted and you'd be sitting in the caboose just gasping," said Larry. Then, as now, marine traffic has the right-of-way and the wait could be up to forty minutes for a train wanting to cross Burrard Inlet. Larry says when he worked for the railway it wouldn't be unusual to take an eighty-car coal train through the tunnel with a crew of four—two in the front and two in the back. "It was pretty hazardous because the engine is spewing stuff and there is only so much the fan could take out of there," he says.

Nowadays, there are two crew members per train, and they sit in the front. It takes up to twenty minutes to clear the exhaust so that there's enough air for the occupants of the next train, limiting use of the tunnel to about two trains an hour. People who live above the tunnel tell me that you can hear a "clickety-clack" or a "banging" sound and feel the vibrations when the trains go through.

THE ROYAL HUDSON MEETS THE AMERICAN FREEDOM TRAIN

On November 1, 1975, the Royal Hudson took 800 passengers on a trip from North Vancouver to Seattle for a meet-up with the steam-powered American Freedom Train, which was on a twenty-one-month tour through forty-eight states. It was the first time a passenger train had crossed the new Second Narrows railroad bridge and travelled through the Thornton Tunnel.

The Royal Hudson exiting the south portal of the Thornton Tunnel.
Angus McIntyre photo, 1975

THE RAILWAY STATIONS OF STATION STREET

By 1919, both the Great Northern Railway and the Canadian National Railway had terminals and rail yards in Vancouver, built on top of landfill taken from development projects in other parts of the city, scrap lumber and bricks from surrounding mills, and general industrial waste.

For nearly half a century the stations of the two competing railways sat side by side. The GNR's Union Station was built first, in 1917, and the CN station followed two years later.

But by the end of the Second World War, rail travel was on the decline, and the GNR offered Union Station to the City of Vancouver for use as a museum and library. The city declined and the station was demolished in 1965. It's been a parking lot ever since, at Station Street and Main, but is slated to become the new home of St. Paul's Hospital.

The CN station's neon sign received a heritage designation in 1980, but less than fifteen years later, the station added a bus terminal, and the sign was taken down and the letters stored in a boxcar at the West Coast Railway Heritage Park in Squamish. The new and current neon sign—Pacific Central—is a made-up name meant to allude to railway history yet remains controversial, mostly because of its tendency to confuse people as to its origins.

TOP View of the CN station under construction and the completed GNR (Union) Station, March 23, 1918.

Vancouver Archives PA-031692 PAN N178

MIDDLE Canadian National Station in 1973.

Vancouver Archives 447-253

BOTTOM Union Station in 1924.

Vancouver Archives Bu N317

THE PNE: PARTY LIKE IT'S 1957

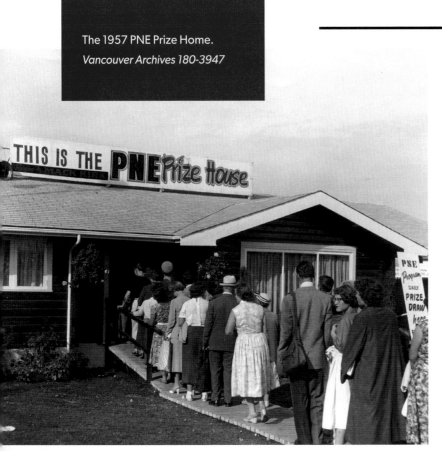

THIS IS THE **PNE** Prize House

In 1957, things were a lot less complicated. People went out to movies and drank Nescafé in the kitchen. The Pacific National Exhibition Prize Home that year was 1,444 square feet. It was a single-storey, boxy, early Ranch-style house and less than half the size of recent prize homes. The house was moved to, and remains at, 6517 Lougheed Highway in Burnaby. It originally sat on a concrete pad, but owners have since added a basement, bringing the total square footage to a little over 2,400.

TEN THINGS YOU WON'T SEE AT THE PNE

1. A BRILL TROLLEY BUS

The first PNE was in 1910, and, not surprisingly, a lot of things have changed since then. Some things will be missed and others not so much. Here are ten things you won't see there anymore.

Unless it's taken out of a transit museum, you won't be taking a Brill trolley bus to the fair. In 1974, Angus McIntyre was riding on the back of a Brill trolley bus that was detoured for the PNE parade at Hastings and Commercial. "There wasn't always a switch or wire for these manoeuvres, so we rode the rear bumper, held onto to a retriever with one hand and pulled both poles down with the other," says Angus, adding that this was done while travelling at speeds of up to twenty miles (thirty kilometres) an hour.

Angus McIntyre riding the back of a Brill trolley bus in 1974.

John Day photo

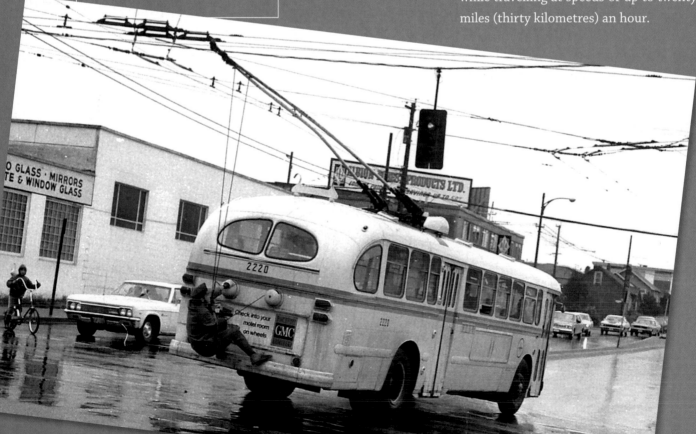

2. THE CHALLENGER RELIEF MAP AND THE BC PAVILION

The BC Pavilion was demolished in 1997, and the Challenger Relief Map of BC that occupied 6,000 square feet (550 square metres) of floor space was placed in storage in an Air Canada hangar at Vancouver International Airport. George Challenger and his family spent seven years building the map of British Columbia to topographical scale from fir plywood cut into 986,000 pieces. It was displayed at the PNE for forty-three years. A section of the map was displayed in the RCMP's Integrated Security Unit office in Richmond but disappeared back into storage once the 2010 Olympic Games ended.

3. A PRIZE HOME UNDER $1 MILLION

The first PNE Prize Home was raffled off in 1934. It was worth $5,000 and is still at 2812 Dundas Street, where it was valued at $1.34 million in 2020. The next house was raffled in 1952, and except for the years 1967 and 1968 when the PNE experimented with $50,000 gold bars, there has been a house raffled off every year since.

TOP The first year of the Challenger Relief Map at the PNE.
Vancouver Archives 180-5614, 1954

BOTTOM The 1934 PNE Prize Home.
Vancouver Archives 180-0597

4. SIDESHOWS

Sideshows were once a huge part of the PNE, especially in the 1940s and '50s. You could pay to see the bearded lady, the man with alligator skin, the four-legged woman or little people on parade. If that wasn't enough, there were girlie revues, palm readers, Siamese twins, and a man with vitiligo (a skin condition that causes white patches).

5. INSPECTOR VANCE'S CRIME LAB

In 1934, Inspector John F.C.B. Vance of the Vancouver Police Department, who was once known as the "Sherlock Holmes of Canada," packed up part of his laboratory and took it on the road. The slogan that Depression year was "Forward British Columbia—Prosperity Beckons," and Vance's display of "scientific apparatus for crime detection"[1] was insured for a whopping $10,000.

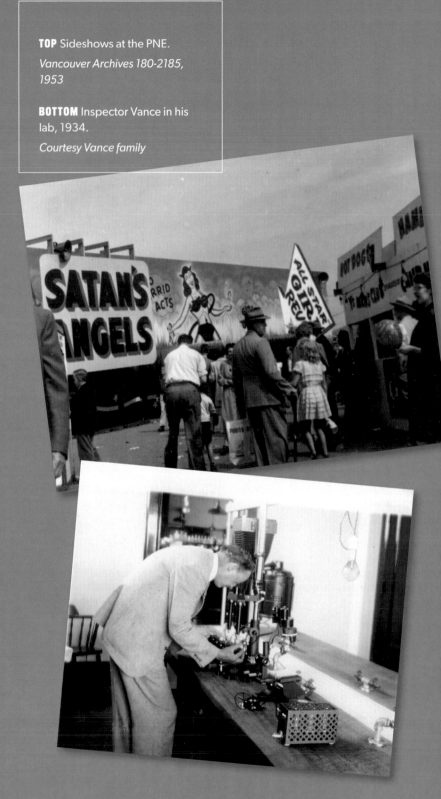

TOP Sideshows at the PNE.
Vancouver Archives 180-2185, 1953

BOTTOM Inspector Vance in his lab, 1934.
Courtesy Vance family

6. DAL RICHARDS

Dal Richards was known as "Vancouver's King of Swing." He was born in 1918 and raised in Marpole. Richards's eleven-piece dance band played at the Hotel Vancouver for twenty-five years, and his radio show, *Dal's Place*, aired for more than two decades. Richards played his seventy-fifth PNE—a seventeen-day run—in 2014. It was his last. He died in December 2015 at age ninety-seven.

7. MISS PNE

That's right, the PNE had beauty queens—forty-three in fact. The last one hung up her crown in 1991, and, personally, I'm not sorry to see them go.

8. A PARADE

The first parade was in 1910, and the last—at least along the route that traversed Georgia, Granville and Hastings Streets—was in 1995. Pictured in 1936 is the Sheet Metal Workers Local 280 rocket on a float. A replica is on permanent display at the south end of the Cambie Street Bridge.

TOP Dal Richards performing at the PNE in 1976. *Vancouver Archives 2010-006-282*

MIDDLE Miss PNE. *Vancouver Archives 180-3218, 1957*

BOTTOM PNE parade. *Vancouver Archives 775-192, 1936*

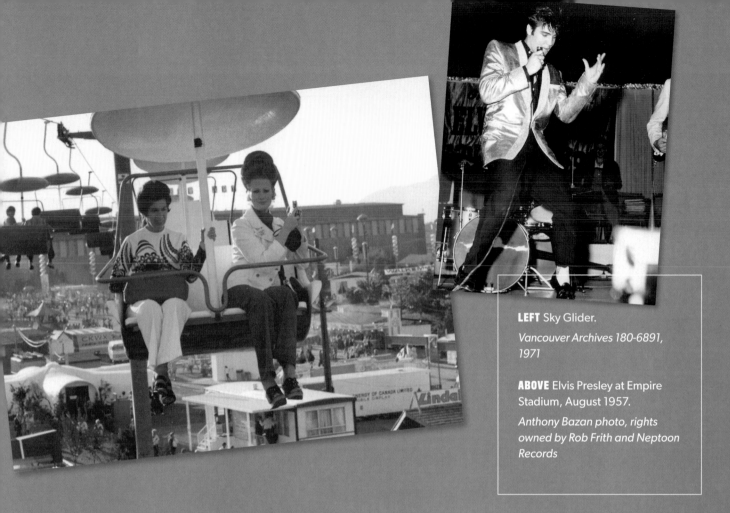

9. SKY GLIDER

The Sky Glider was a ride introduced to the PNE in 1970 and was a crowd favourite for fifteen years. It carried passengers in gondola chairs suspended from a steel cable in a seven-minute one-way trip. The ride ran almost the full length of the fairgrounds, from the entrance to the roller coaster to a station near the old Showmart Building exhibit hall. If you're wondering where it went, you can check it out at Mount Seymour—it's been the Brockton Chair since 1988.

10. ELVIS PRESLEY AND EMPIRE STADIUM

We had Elvis Presley. It's true. He only performed three shows outside of the United States—Toronto, Montreal and Vancouver. In August 1957, more than 26,000 fans paid $3.75 each to see him at Empire Stadium, which was constructed in 1954 for the British Empire and Commonwealth Games. It was home to the BC Lions football team from 1954 to 1982, then demolished in 1993.

THE LIVESTOCK BUILDING AT HASTINGS PARK

Most of us know the Livestock Building from taking our kids to the petting zoo and the pig races and to see Big Bob the bull at the annual PNE. It's an old concrete warehouse, covered in peeling paint. Each year it looks a little more run-down, and each year there is talk of renovation, seismic reinforcements and infrastructure upgrades. The back is just as neglected, painted red from a very old film shoot.

Although the building is in need of a facelift, it is one of four that are still standing on the fairgrounds that have a social history that we should never forget.

These buildings—the others are the Forum, the Pure Foods Building (Rollerland) and the Garden Auditorium—are important for their architectural merit, but more vitally, they serve as a reminder of the injustice suffered by 22,000 Japanese Canadians during the Second World War. From March to September 1942, more than 8,000 Japanese Canadians passed through Hastings Park on their way to internment camps. Families were separated by gender and age, and they were put in deplorable living conditions.

The first part of the Livestock Building went up in 1929, and then in the '40s, architectural firm McCarter Nairne, the same firm that designed the Marine Building, turned it into a much larger, Streamline Moderne building. During the war, Japanese Canadian women and children were placed in the animal stalls at the western end of the building. The eastern section housed a hospital, kitchen and dining area. Muriel (Fujiwara) Kitagawa described the Japanese women's dormitory: "The whole place is impregnated with the smell of ancient manure and maggots. Every other day it is swept with dichlorine of lime, or something, but you can't disguise horse smell, cow smell, sheep, pigs, rabbits and goats ... there are 10 showers for 1,500 women."[2]

The Pure Foods Building, built in 1931, was turned into a dormitory for teenage boys, while the Forum, built in 1933 as the Automotive and Ice Rink Building, housed men over eighteen. The Garden Auditorium, designed in 1939 as a dance hall by Townley and Matheson, the same architects who designed city hall, became the classroom for hundreds of Japanese Canadian kids.

All of these men, women and children were declared "enemy aliens," wrenched from their homes and sent to live here before being forcibly relocated to internment camps in places like BC's Slocan Valley. Everything they owned—houses, cars, boats—was confiscated and sold.

TOP Livestock Building, 2020.
Eve Lazarus photo

BOTTOM Forum Building, 2020.
Eve Lazarus photo

KINGSGATE
MALL

The thing about Kingsgate Mall on East Broadway is you either love it or you hate it. It's weird or wonderful, strange or quaint, creepy or quirky, but it rarely goes unnoticed. The cupola has turned the mall into a landmark, but I can't imagine calling it a destination by any stretch of the imagination. Aside from a dental surgery and a credit union, one of the only stores not found in most other shopping malls is the Lolli Pretty Clothing Company, which has the fabulous tagline, "Your Candy Store of Fashion."

When the mall was built in 1974, it took the place of Mount Pleasant School, an eighty-year-old solid brick building built in 1892 that was originally known as False Creek School. The land underneath the mall is owned by the Vancouver School Board and has been since the late 1880s. The VSB, in turn, leases the land to Beedie Development Group, and they operate the

mall. It's no surprise that Beedie would like to buy the mall, pull it down and redevelop the land. Perhaps the pinned tweet on the unofficial Kingsgate Mall Twitter account says it all: "STILL NOT A CONDO."

Kingsgate Mall.
Eve Lazarus photo, 2020

1 Windows from Mount Pleasant School.
   Angus McIntyre photo

2 Mount Pleasant School was demolished
   in 1972 to make way for Kingsgate Mall.
   Vancouver Archives Sch P33, 1902

3 Mount Pleasant School, 1972.
   Angus McIntyre photo

4 The original 1892 blackboard at Mount
   Pleasant School was uncovered shortly
   before the building was demolished
   in the early 1970s.
   Angus McIntyre photo

5 The 1892 blackboard.
   Angus McIntyre photo

A (MOSTLY) WORKING MAN'S MURAL

Looking at the outside of the plain two-storey building at Victoria Drive and Triumph Street, you'd never guess that it houses a colourful mural that runs the full length of an eighty-two-foot (twenty-five-metre) wall. The building is the home of the Maritime Labour Centre, and Fraser Wilson painted the mural in 1947, the same year that he was fired after speaking out against management at the start of a brutal newspaper strike that went on for more than three years.

An illustrator and cartoonist for the *Vancouver Sun* for ten years, Wilson told a reporter in 1991 that a statement was read to him that said he was being dismissed for disloyalty to the paper and had an hour to leave the premises.

In 1947, Wilson was the forty-two-year-old president of the newspaper guild, and probably because of that, he was hired to paint a mural honouring BC workers and their contributions to industry onto the walls of the Boilermaker's Hall on West Pender Street. For the next four decades, the Pender Auditorium, as it was known, became the venue for a number of bands, including the Grateful Dead in 1966. When the building sold in 1985, the new owner wanted to divide the main hall into offices. It would have been the end of the mural, which had been painted directly onto the Gyproc. Instead, a deal was struck to move it to the new union building on Triumph Street.

The mural was taken down in sheets, scraped off the plaster backing, glued to heavy canvas and then onto birch plywood and, finally, cut into small panels. Fred Svensson, a retired shipwright and joiner, is one of the few members of Marine Workers' and Boilermakers' Industrial

Union Local 1 who remembers the mural in its original setting. Unfortunately, the wall in the new building was more than fifteen feet (4.5 metres) shorter than the old wall. "They took out the section right in the middle," says Svensson. "There's two trees in the centre of it now. It looks a little odd, but it doesn't take away from the picture."

He's right—the mural is stunning. Wilson was eighty-three when the mural was moved to the Maritime Labour Centre in 1988, and he was still running his graphic design business. He returned to paint the transition scenes, and the lost panels were probably discarded, says Fred. Lucky it was moved, because the Pender Auditorium burned down in 2003. The mural has so far survived a couple of fires in the new building and an attempt to sell the building that the membership managed to stave off.

LEFT Fraser Wilson at work on his mural, 1985.
SFU Digital Library MSC179-33130

BELOW Fraser Wilson's mural at the Maritime Labour Centre.
Eve Lazarus photo, 2020

THE INFANT MEMORIAL GARDEN AT MOUNTAIN VIEW CEMETERY

The Infant Memorial Garden at Mountain View Cemetery.

Elsa Brobbey photo, courtesy LEES+Associates

Mountain View Cemetery opened in 1886. Over the years, five parcels of land were added to the original property, until the cemetery was just over 100 acres (forty hectares). Presently, about 150,000 people occupy the space, either through burial or cremation, 251 of whom remain unidentified.

Between 1907 and 1972, nearly 11,000 babies were buried in unmarked graves at Mountain View Cemetery. Some of the babies died at birth, others lived for a few hours or a few days. Few had markers or graveside ceremonies.

Parents were expected to suck it up, go home and make more babies.

In 2006, Glen Hodges, cemetery manager, spearheaded the creation of a garden that would give the babies back their identities, and their parents a special place to grieve.

The Infant Memorial Garden is just a short walk from the cemetery's main office, a spot chosen because that particular piece of ground, known as Jones Section Block 18, was the biggest of the common grave areas, the size of ten burial plots.

A boulder marks the entrance to the garden, and it is inscribed and dedicated to the families. The garden is designed around a stream bed filled with 6,610 stones, each representing one of the tiny bodies that are buried here. More than 100 families have bought a commemorative stone with the name of their baby and date of their death. And the inscriptions are heartbreaking. There's Baby Girl Quackenbush, April 19, 1934. Beeson Beloved Son was born and died on Christmas Eve, 1940. There is a marble square in the grass dedicated to Baby Stark, June 16, 1956. Theresa and Josephine Carolet were twins who were born and died over two days in May 1962.

Before the memorial garden went in, the cemetery often received calls from grieving families who had lost a child thirty, forty or even fifty years prior. "When they asked if they could put a marker there, we had to say no," says Glen. "Now we can say yes, and here's how you do it."

Memorial boulder at the entrance to the Infant Memorial Garden at Mountain View Cemetery.

Wayne Worden photo

TOMBSTONES

In 2015, Rena Del Pieve Gobbi came under fire in the media for using discarded gravestones to hold up her garden, which was wedged in between the Maple Leaf Self Storage and the train tracks at Commercial Drive and Powell Street. Rena, an artist and documentary filmmaker, then lived at the artist resource centre just across from the garden.

The stones were rejects from Mountain View Cemetery. They were cracked and peeling and in bad shape. Rena found that quite disturbing. "I deliberated over it for a day before I did it, and I made a very conscious decision to place the gravestones with the names facing out," she says. "I really felt it was disrespectful to people to face their names to the dirt."

Rena started to build her garden in 2007 around the eight discarded gravestones. That was the year that the trial was underway for serial killer Robert Pickton, and for Rena, the garden became a kind of tribute to all the women of the Downtown Eastside who were ignored and murdered. "I live in an industrial wasteland," she said at the time. "I've taken every single place that you can put dirt around my building and made a garden of it."

Rena isn't the only person to repurpose gravestones: the parks board has been doing it for decades. By the 1960s, many of the old upright monuments at Mountain View Cemetery had come loose and were often found knocked over, vandalized and otherwise desecrated. A decision was made to lay the inscribed stones flush in the ground and remove the granite bases that held them upright. Cemetery manager Glen Hodges figures that could have involved up to 8,000 monuments. Some

Rena Del Pieve Gobbi's gravestone garden.
Rena Del Pieve Gobbi photo, 2015

of the granite bases were repurposed in a retaining wall for the cemetery on Fraser Street, and thousands of bases from military graves were trucked to Stanley Park for use in the seawall.

Some of the stones that were inscribed were discarded or damaged, or they were ones that had been replaced by family members of the deceased. These stones were turned inward so the names were not visible. Glen says it's not unusual for families to replace gravestones. Sometimes they want to add another name, and there's no room on the existing stone, so the old stone needs to be replaced. The discarded stones were piled up in a big storage yard at the cemetery and later relocated to an area near the Fraser retaining wall. "It wouldn't be uncommon for someone who was looking for a little patio stone and wandered through the cemetery to just take one," he says. "The cemetery is a public place. We can't lock everything up."

THE INDUSTRIAL SCHOOL FOR GIRLS

A replica of the original turret on the renovated building where girls were once locked up for punishment.

Eve Lazarus photo, 2020

In 1954, seventeen-year-old Gay Turner was tossed into the Provincial Industrial School for Girls for being drunk. On her first day she was taken to the superintendent's office and told to shut her mouth, behave herself and take a hairdressing course. The next day she escaped with another girl. "We got drunk and we got caught and we got brought back," she told me.

It was New Year's Eve, and she was locked in the cupola on the roof by herself. "I remember crying and listening to all of Vancouver and I could hear the bells and I heard people yelling 'Happy New Year' everywhere."

Gay broke one of the panes of glass and slashed at her wrists. The damage was minimal, but she was thrown in the "hole" in the basement. A girl started yelling and others joined in. Soon they were breaking windows and making a lot of noise. "And you know what they did on a winter evening in these unheated cells? They used firehoses, real firehoses," she says. "One girl was soaked down and left all night and ended up with pneumonia. An ambulance came for her the next day."

Gay freely admits to being a teenage alcoholic. It was a common offence of the inmates, but so was running away from a violent home, being an orphan or being Indigenous when the residential schools were filled beyond capacity. The minimum sentence for any charge was six months, and by the time Gay arrived, the girls ranged in age from eight to eighteen.

Gay was luckier than most. A sponsor from Alcoholics Anonymous helped get her transferred to Oakalla Prison. "I was ten times better treated," she says. "I could rave about people who ran that place. I saw some humanity." Gay spent four months there.

The Provincial Industrial School for Girls opened at 868 Cassiar Street in 1914, for "the education, industrial training and moral reclamation" of girls under sixteen convicted of an offence punishable by imprisonment. The building was surrounded by fourteen acres (six hectares) and located on the outskirts of the city in Hastings Townsite. By 1918, it was walled up behind a six-foot-high fence.

In November 1954, the month before Gay was incarcerated, a report was issued to the provincial health minister. It told of dungeon-like cells with girls sleeping on mattresses and blankets tossed on damp floors. The report noted that all prisoners were lumped together: runaways, prostitutes, those with addictions, mental illness and cognitive disabilities. "Our Girls' Industrial School makes Kingston's prison for women look like a luxury hotel," wrote *Province* reporter Jean Howarth in 1954. "The women at Kingston have better quarters, more privileges, far more opportunities to pick up a hobby or learn a trade and are treated with infinitely less harshness than the children on Cassiar. Kingston is not good; but the Girls' Industrial School is an evil horror."

Howarth found seven of the thirty girls in the "holes" in the basement; one twelve-year-old had been there for six weeks. "The whole place is reminiscent of an insane asylum about the turn of the century," she wrote.[3] Two years later, nothing had changed and the *Vancouver Sun*'s Simma Holt was sent to report on the school. She called it a "house of horror."[4]

The Cassiar Street institution closed in 1959, after forty-five years of operation, and the girls were moved to a new building on Willingdon Avenue in Burnaby. The Cassiar facility was used for provincial government offices until 1995, when it was converted into twelve residential units and surrounded by a seventy-six-unit townhouse development.

Gay is now a great-grandmother and has been sober since 1992.

CITY OF VANCOUVER

HERITAGE BUILDING

PROVINCIAL INDUSTRIAL HOME FOR GIRLS

Architect: A. Arthur Cox

This building was designed in 1912 and opened in 1914 as a girls' vocational school. With its arcaded porch, curvilinear parapets, and moulded window trim, it is one of the city's most distinguished examples of the Mission Revival style. The conversion to 12 residential units by United Properties Ltd., was based on a design by McGinn Engineering and Preservation Ltd. and involved the replacement of the central cupola. In addition, new windows were installed based on the original design. The development also includes seven new buildings, designed by H.R. Hatch Architect Ltd. to be compatible with the original structure.

RIGHT Heritage plaque outside 868 Cassiar Street.

Eve Lazarus, 2020

BELOW The former Provincial Industrial School for Girls is now an upmarket residential building.

Eve Lazarus, 2020

CHEF CHUCK CURRIE'S POLKA-DOT HOUSE

Several years ago, I heard about a white house with red polka dots on the corner of East Third Avenue and Lakewood Drive. It sounded fabulous, so I drove over to take a look. I knocked on the door and was astounded to have Chuck Currie, who at the time was executive chef of White Spot restaurants, answer the door in his working whites. He was just like the celebrity chef he played in the television commercials.

Chuck, who has lived in the house since 1989, and first painted the polka dots with marine paint in 1992, says there's no big story. His friend John Cobourne was working for a painting company, and his boss went on holiday and came home to find that his crew had painted his house with purple polka dots. The owner wasn't amused, but Chuck loved the idea and thought it was a great way to liven up his own neighbourhood. The neighbourhood, incidentally, is packed full of gorgeous old heritage houses.

He's never had a single complaint.

"I still remember the first car that stopped and gaped. It was a cool fall day and the windows were closed, but my friend John and I could clearly see the driver say, 'Holy shit!'" I had a sax quartet rehearsal here that Sunday and one of the musicians said he had been talking to a friend in Toronto who asked him, 'Say, have you heard about that polka-dot house in Vancouver?' That was five days after we painted it!"

In the ensuing years, Chuck has heard it described as the house with measles, and two little girls from the neighbourhood thought it looked like a ladybug. Another benefit is the paint job seems to attract hummingbirds. John Cobourne is now

a top restorer of fine yachts on the West Coast, but he still returns to help Chuck repaint his house every few years.

Chef Chuck, who can rustle up a mean ravioli—he opened up the first Earls restaurant in 1982—left White Spot in 2014, but he still lives in the house. He also plays and teaches saxophone and clarinet. He says the great thing about his house is that students find it easily. And he's always coming home to find anonymous gifts on his doorstep—bowls, juice pitchers, coffee mugs—all with polka dots, of course.

TOP LEFT Chef Chuck Currie, 2013. *Eve Lazarus photo*

TOP RIGHT Chuck Currie's house from the back. *Courtesy Chuck Currie*

LEFT Chuck Currie's house at Lakewood and East Third Avenue. *Courtesy Chuck Currie*

THE VANTAN NUDIST CLUB

I've lived on the North Shore for more than twenty years, and although I'd heard rumours of a nudist camp at the top of Mountain Highway, I always thought it was an urban myth.

Turns out, it's not. The VanTan Nudist Club has about fifty members. The club has a website and a board of directors, just like any other non-profit society—they're just naked when they meet. They even enter a float in the Lynn Valley Days parade every year and host a couple of open houses in the summer.

I fired off an email to Daniel Jackson, VanTan's PR guy, and was invited to spend a summer afternoon there. Not surprisingly, the area that's owned by the nudist camp is quite secluded. The day I went, Daniel and his partner, Vanessa, met me at the first locked gate, which is just past the public parking lot. We drove about a mile (two kilometres) up a curvy, unpaved road that was shared by a steady stream of determined mountain bikers and hikers, through another locked gate, and then onto several acres of private property.

VanTan was founded in 1939, making it Canada's oldest nudist club. In the 1930s, the District of North Vancouver surveyed the land at the top of Mountain Highway all the way to the Grouse Mountain Chalet and carved it up into half-acre lots. A VanTan member bought three lots and sold them to the club in 1945. The club leased another three lots from the district to maintain their privacy and bought another two lots along the bluff from a group called the Millionaires' Club, which used the land for clay pigeon shooting. There were no electricity, water or sewage connections (there still aren't), and the proposed subdivision never took off.

From the VanTan
historical album.

*Courtesy VanTan
Nudist Club*

The club's buildings—which include a sauna inside a log cabin with a hand-split cedar roof—date back to the 1940s and '50s. There's a fire-suppression reservoir, which holds 10,500 gallons (40,000 litres) of water and doubles as a swimming pool. There's a shower, diesel backup generator, composting toilet and propane heater. At the bottom of the property is a stunning view of Mount Baker, Mount Seymour and Burrard Inlet.

While they could always use a few new members, Daniel says reaching out to the community is more about changing their image. "[The media] still play off, 'there's something going on up there and it's not wholesome,'" he says. In fact, most of the club's secrecy surrounds individual privacy. Members don't talk about what they do, where they live or mention their last names. And membership is intentionally cheap—just a few hundred dollars a year. Members are asked to put in ten hours of work a year, but it's all pretty casual. You can chop wood for the sauna and hot tub, work in the community garden or on trail maintenance, but it's not *Survivor*—if you just want to sit by the swimming pool, no one's going to kick you off the mountain.

"I always say it's the secret that keeps itself. Once you've come and had a look, really, nothing out of the ordinary is taking place here," says Daniel. "Gardening is the number one activity." And, yes, after a few uncomfortable minutes of holding extreme eye contact, the whole nudity thing becomes a very small deal. It's a bit like hanging out with a very pleasant middle-aged naked gardening group.

VanTan Nudist Club.
Eve Lazarus photos, 2016

FRED HOLLINGSWORTH'S SKY BUNGALOW

I'm a huge fan of West Coast Modern architecture, which developed here in the 1940s, a time when it was thought that it was more important to blend a house into its surroundings than impose itself upon them. People are often surprised to learn that our stock of rapidly disappearing mid-century modern houses designed by architects such as Arthur Erickson, Barry Downs, Ron Thom and Paul Merrick are considered heritage, and many of those that are left are listed in heritage registers.

Fred Thornton Hollingsworth was a rock star when it came to designing houses from post-and-beam construction, often with a small footprint and open plan that used glass and western red cedar to bring natural light and views of nature into the house. As early as 1946, Hollingsworth was including radiant floor heating, clerestory windows and skylights to let in lots of light. His houses are part design, part art and part architecture.

"Boxes are a symbol of containment," he told a *Vancouver Sun* reporter in 1998. "They aren't suitable for human occupation. You're boxed in. We tried to open the buildings up to the landscape while providing privacy."[1]

Hollingsworth died in 2015 at age ninety-eight. He still lived in the same North Vancouver West Coast Modern house that he designed for his family in 1946, just blocks away from another of his designs—the Sky Bungalow.

The amazing thing about the Sky Bungalow—apart from the fact that it exists at all—is that it started life in a downtown parking lot. In 1949, Eric Allan, a property developer, came up with the idea of building a house in the Hudson's

Sky Bungalow, 3355 Aintree Drive, North Vancouver.
Eve Lazarus photo, 2020

Bay store parking lot to promote the new Capilano Highlands subdivision. The Bay agreed—but only if the house took up no more than six parking spots. No problem, said Hollingsworth. He perched the wooden house on brick columns and floated it over the cars.

The Sky Bungalow was a huge hit. Thousands of people paid ten cents to tour the house—and the money was donated to the Vancouver Symphony Orchestra.

The house sold and was barged across Burrard Inlet in 1950 to its current address at 3355 Aintree Drive in North Vancouver, where it is surrounded by contemporary bungalows that have so far stayed with the scale and the feel of the neighbourhood.

THE BC MILLS HOUSE MUSEUM, A MYSTERY, A CAPTAIN AND A TROLL

BC Mills House Museum at Lynn Headwaters.

Eve Lazarus photo, 2020

If you're hiking at Lynn Headwaters Regional Park, you'll see the little green house with yellow trim, just past the parking lot. The two-bedroom house was purchased from a catalogue in 1908 by Captain Henry Pybus and originally located at East First Street, near Lonsdale Avenue.

It was a prefab Model J house constructed by the BC Mills Timber and Trading Company, which operated out of what's now the Mission to Seafarers house at the foot of Dunlevy Avenue. The house's most famous resident was Richard "the Troll" Schaller, former leader of the Rhinoceros Party of Canada, which ran candidates between 1963 and 1993 on the promise "to keep none of our promises." Other platforms included promises to "repeal the law of gravity," "provide higher education by building taller schools" and "ban guns and butter—both kill."

In 1995, the house was saved from demolition and moved to its present location at Lynn Headwaters. The Coronado, a four-storey condo building, is now in its former location.

BRING BACK THE STREETCAR!

On September 3, 1906, the first North Vancouver streetcar began its journey at the ferry dock, travelled up Lonsdale Avenue and stopped at Twelfth Street. Jack Kelly was the conductor aboard that inaugural run. Everything went smoothly on the way up, but on the way back down, the brakes failed and Car 25 came crashing into another streetcar waiting at the bottom of the hill.

Three years later, Kelly was at the controls of Car 62 when it headed down Lonsdale Avenue to meet the four p.m. ferry. Once again, the brakes failed. With fifteen passengers screaming in fright, including the mayor's wife, the car careened down the hill and right off the end of the dock. Kelly leaped from the car, breaking his leg. All of the passengers were fished out of the harbour.

Car 153 was built by the J.G. Brill Company of Philadelphia and motored up and down Lonsdale Avenue for thirty-five years. It was designed as a double-ender, so when it reached the Windsor Road terminus at the top of Lonsdale, the motorman and the conductor switched places for the return trip and flipped the trolley pole the other way. When North Vancouver discontinued streetcars in 1947, most of their parts were sold off for scrap, while a few became summer cottages or farm buildings. Car 153 survived first as a motel cabin near Mission, then as a restaurant in Chilliwack and, finally, as a chicken coop on a Fraser Valley farm, where it was rediscovered in 1982. Car 153 was restored and is now back at the foot of Lonsdale, in the new North Vancouver Museum and Archives building.

A streetcar meets the Brill trolley bus that will soon replace it at the foot of Lonsdale Avenue, ca. 1947.

NVMA 6453

THE SEVEN SEAS RESTAURANT

RIGHT The Seven Seas restaurant, ca. 1970s.
NVMA 15806

BELOW Ferry No. 5 crossing Burrard Inlet, 1958.
Vancouver Archives 447-7232.1

Most North Vancouver residents will remember the Seven Seas, a restaurant that was moored at the foot of Lonsdale Avenue between 1959 and 2002. Some may even remember it as Norvan Ferry No. 5, a forerunner to the SeaBus, and one of the vessels that ferried people between Vancouver and the North Shore. Ferry No. 5 went into service in 1941 and could carry up to 600 people and thirty vehicles across Burrard Inlet.

Harry Almas, who owned the King Neptune Seafoods restaurant in New Westminster, bought the ferry from the City of North Vancouver in 1959, a year after the ferries took their last run across the inlet. He paid $12,000, which included a five-year lease for the waterfront lot. He then spent ten times the purchase price converting the car deck into two dining rooms and a kitchen. Almas kept the two wheelhouses on the upper deck and the ship's funnel.

The restaurant had a huge neon sign that was easily visible from East Vancouver, and it was the place where many locals had their first drink, got engaged and ate at the city's biggest seafood buffet.

Jeanne Nielsen remembers taking the ferry from Vancouver with her grandmother when she was nine years old. "It was really an

adventure. I just loved going. It was a big deal," she says. When Ferry No. 5 became the Seven Seas restaurant, Jeanne went there with her friends. "We used to think it was fantastic. I remember us going there in our late teens and early twenties and having this incredible seafood buffet—they even had frog legs."

The ship's heritage significance was recognized on the Heritage Inventory in 1994, but the vessel was aging, and the cost of repairs became a court battle between the Almas family and the city. It ended in federal court in 2001. The following year the restaurant was dismantled, towed to Vancouver Pile Driving at the foot of Brooksbank Avenue and demolished.

The neon sign was lost to history.

ST. PAUL'S INDIAN RESIDENTIAL SCHOOL

In 2016, I was hired by the North Vancouver Museum and Archives to work with a team on an interactive exhibit called *Water's Edge*. It was a dream job, where I put together the framework for the exhibit then researched and wrote more than 100 different stories. Although a lot of the information was new to me, there was one story in particular that shocked me: North Vancouver had a residential school. It was on Keith Road, where the private Catholic high school St. Thomas Aquinas is today.

NVMA has collected a wealth of information on the former residential school, including photos and hours and hours of taped interviews with some of the survivors. St. Paul's Indian Residential School was one of eighteen such schools in the province and the closest to Vancouver. It was originally built in 1899 as a day school for children from the Squamish Nation, and then turned into a government-funded, church-run institution. Under this plan of aggressive assimilation, children as young as three were forcibly removed from their homes and sent to residential schools where their "education" mostly consisted of English lessons and where they were force-fed Christianity. Their languages and cultures were literally beaten out of them.

St. Paul's Residential School
boxing team, ca. 1950.
NVMA 4791

St. Paul's Residential
School, ca. 1920.
NVMA 11417

A report by the Truth and Reconciliation Commission of Canada in 2015 called the residential school system cultural genocide.

In August 1909, the *Province* sent a reporter to interview Father Edward Peytavin, an Oblate priest and head of the residential school. "On the hillside is seen the school where 10 sisters strive to instill some idea of the arts of civilization in the minds of the little Indians," noted the reporter. "The children live at the school, and are under surveillance all the time."[2]

Father Peytavin told the reporter that "the results are pitifully small."

"The boys become fishermen, idle and shiftless as their elders, and the girls become wives of fishermen, and household slatterns. What else can they do poor things," said the father. "Sometimes I wonder whether we are really accomplishing anything at all. But that is not the spirit we must bring to a labour of this kind. We must keep on working, hoping, praying."[3]

The girls were taught cooking, dressmaking, housework and lace making, while the boys worked in the garden, painted and did general carpentry around the school site.

During the Depression, St. Paul's was a particularly bleak place to be. Government officials reported that the school was a "death-trap," with children being half-starved, and with outbreaks of influenza, chicken pox and smallpox.[4]

On his sixth birthday, William Nahanee was sent to St. Paul's, just like his father before him. "We all had numbers. We weren't referred to by name," he recalls. "There was a lot of time spent in religious instruction and praying. I found out later, the sisters in that school did not come with teaching certificates. They were learning on the job." He remembers being hauled out of bed by two of the sisters and given 100 lashes on his bottom with a leather strap. "Some of my brothers were there, and they counted," All of the male children who were medically fit, he says, were forced to box. In 1950, he and his brother were taken to the BC Penitentiary in New Westminster for a boxing match. The prisoners were dressed in coveralls, and they clapped and yahooed at the boys, says Nahanee. "Me and my brother went out and we did a good show for them."[5]

St. Paul's Indian Residential School was demolished in 1959, and the red building of the first St. Thomas Aquinas Secondary School—and now slated for demolition—rose in its place.

THE SURVIVORS' MONUMENT

A monument dedicated to residential school survivors was installed in 2014.

Eve Lazarus photo, 2020

In 2014, a monument was installed at the corner of Forbes Avenue and Sixth Street, in front of the old convent, looking down on the site of the former residential school. The monument depicts two children in a canoe riding toward the crest of a wave. The wave going up represents Indigenous people regaining their language and culture. The other section of the wave, which starts at a high point and then dips down into a depression, represents Indigenous people's contact with Europeans, which resulted in their freedom and culture being stripped away from them. The monument was carved by Jason Nahanee, a residential school survivor who was sent there at age three, and is dedicated to the more than 2,000 mostly Coast Salish people who were confined there.

The monument was a collaboration between the Squamish Nation, the Roman Catholic Archdiocese of Vancouver, the Sisters of the Child Jesus, the Assembly of First Nations and the City and District of North Vancouver.

THE UNSOLVED RAPE AND MURDER OF ALBINA LEQUIEA

On Sunday, December 16, 1973, ninety-six-year-old Albina Christiana Lequiea was found dead in her bed on the second floor of the North Vancouver convent.

At first, it was thought that she had died from natural causes, but when her body was examined at Lions Gate Hospital, they found that she had been raped and strangled with a nylon stocking. She was still wearing her pink nightgown.

The building is still there at 524 West Sixth Street, but the sisters have since moved, and it's now part of St. Thomas Aquinas Secondary School.

In 1973, when Lequiea was a resident, the convent also served as a home for the elderly. After the murder, one of the nuns told police that she had found a man in his early twenties wandering inside the convent at around 3:30 in the morning.

He had a beard and shoulder-length dirty blond hair. He wore jeans, had striking eyes and reeked of booze. He said to her: "Where's the door? How do I get out?"[6] After he left, she reported the sighting to her superior but not to the police. Later, they found that he had got in by smashing a glass panel in the front door.

The articles—a total of sixteen news stories—that were published during the time between her murder in 1973 and the last one in 2000 all focused on a "psychopathic killer"; there was nothing in them about Lequiea's long life. I went searching for a death certificate to find out where she was born. Instead, I found a magazine article written in 2007 by Elizabeth Withey, Lequiea's great-granddaughter.

According to Withey, Lequiea was born Albina Christiana Proulx in Nicolet, Quebec, in 1877. When she was nineteen, she married Phillip Lequiea, and they raised nine children on a farm near Battleford, Saskatchewan. Lequiea was a "fervent catholic" who was "tiny, gentle and devoted to her family and God."[7] She went to church every morning before breakfast, and it must have made her happy that one of her sons became a priest. Ed Lequiea led the funeral mass for his mother.

Even with the description from the nun who'd seen the young man, and a composite drawing that ran in the newspapers, Lequiea's murderer was never found. His description sounds remarkably like the one that was given to police after the murder of sixteen-year-old Rhona Duncan less than three years later. Duncan had been raped and strangled on her way home from a party at West Fifteenth Street and Bewicke Avenue, just blocks from the convent.

The murders of Albina Lequiea and Rhona Duncan are two of North Vancouver's seventeen unsolved cases dating back to 1964. After 2003, new investigations were transferred to IHIT—the RCMP's Integrated Homicide Investigation Team.

The former convent on West Sixth Street.
Eve Lazarus photo, 2020

THE CAPILANO AIR PARK

Wedged between Pemberton Avenue and Lower Capilano Road, just east of the Lions Gate Bridge, Norgate is one of the few areas that is yet to see massive change to its housing stock—a collection of tidy, modestly sized mid-century ranchers with big gardens. The whole area has a kind of *Leave It to Beaver* 1950s feel with streets named after trees such as Rosewood, Dogwood, Maplewood and Alderwood. It's also one of the few flat areas of North Vancouver—a reason why the land was originally planned to become the Capilano Air Park. The new airfield was first proposed in 1945, and the idea was that it would include luxury accommodation and cater to tourists flying their own planes from other parts of North America. In the end, North Vancouver couldn't afford it, and the land was sold to a developer that modelled Norgate after a typical California subdivision, building houses fifty at a time from a nearby mill.

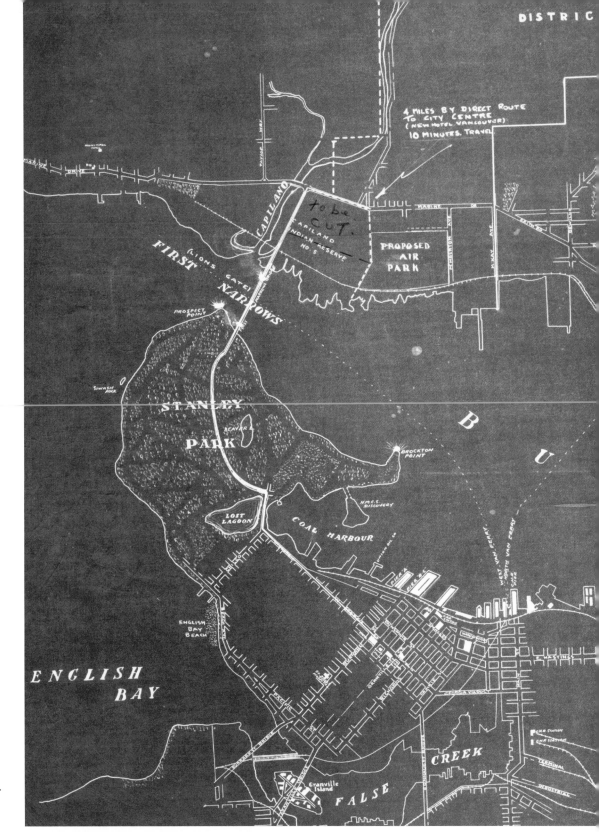

LEFT A typical Norgate rancher.
Eve Lazarus photo, 2020

RIGHT Map showing the proposed Capilano Air Park, ca. 1945.
NVMA

Text on map:

DISTRIC

4 MILES BY DIRECT ROUTE
TO CITY CENTRE
(NEW HOTEL VANCOUVER)
10 MINUTES. TRAVEL

to be CUT.

PROPOSED AIR PARK

CAPILANO INDIAN RESERVE NO 5

FIRST NARROWS
(LIONS GATE)

PROSPECT POINT

SIWASH ROCK

STANLEY PARK

BEAVER L.

BROCKTON POINT

B U

LOST LAGOON

H.M.C.S. DISCOVERY

COAL HARBOUR

ENGLISH BAY BEACH

ENGLISH BAY

WEST VAN. FERRY
NORTH VAN FERRY

Granville Island

FALSE CREEK

THE TOMAHAWK BARBECUE RESTAURANT

Chief Mathias Joe shown in front of the totem pole he carved for the original Tomahawk restaurant on Marine Drive, since moved to the current location on Philip Avenue and repainted by his grandson.
NVMA 9988

In 2000, I signed a contract with a Toronto publisher to write *Frommer's with Kids Vancouver*. I was a freelance journalist with three kids under eight, and part of the job was to road-test every activity and restaurant and side trip that would be included in the book. After the first week, my kids were begging to stay home. But I remember they really enjoyed the Tomahawk restaurant. And why wouldn't they?

The Tomahawk was founded in 1926 by Chick Chamberlain and is now in the hands of his son Chuck and in its third location. Part restaurant and part museum, the building is filled with woodcarvings, masks, small totem poles, woven cedar baskets, hatchets, pots and drums. Some of the items date back to the Depression, when Chick had a close relationship with First Nations people and traded food for handicrafts.

ABOVE LEFT
Tomahawk restaurant,
1550 Philip Avenue.
*Eve Lazarus photo,
2020*

ABOVE RIGHT
Tomahawk restaurant
menu.
Eve Lazarus collection

The totem poles out front were carved by Chief Mathias Joe for the original restaurant on Marine Drive, and the restaurant celebrates its Indigenous connections with burgers named after Chiefs Joe Capilano, Simon Baker, August Jack, and others.

CBC broadcaster Grant Lawrence's band the Smugglers launched their tenth-anniversary album at the Tomahawk in 1998. They'd formed the band while attending West Vancouver's Hillside Secondary School. According to local lore, another rocker and North Van high school student—Bryan Adams—washed dishes there.

TOM BUTLER, THE COACH HOUSE INN AND THE BELLY FLOP THAT SOARED

It's hard to fathom how anyone could think that a belly flop competition was a good idea, but Tom Butler did back in the 1970s—as it happens, he was right. Former *Vancouver Sun* reporter turned PR guy, Butler was the master of the photo op. He once borrowed a beaver from the Stanley Park Zoo for a cross-US tour to promote local tourism.[8] According to a *Globe and Mail* story from 1979: "The beaver scrambled up the steps of San Francisco City Hall to be hugged by the mayor, and promptly committed an indignity of relieving itself." The front-page caption in the next day's paper was "Damn That Beaver."

Butler talked astronaut Neil Armstrong into coming to Vancouver and opening a revolving restaurant above the Sears Tower (now Harbour Centre). The slogan for the event: "The restaurant that soars halfway to the moon in the night sky over Vancouver was opened by a man who went all the way."

But back to belly flops. Butler invented the World Belly Flop and Cannonball Diving Championship in 1975 to publicize the Bayshore Hotel's new pool. That first year, top billing went to seven-foot-four (2.2-metre) professional wrestler André the Giant, later immortalized for his performance as Fezzik in *The Princess Bride*. In 1976, the American Hotel and Motel Association recognized the belly flop competition as North America's best publicity stunt for that year.

After that, the competition moved to the Coach House Inn in North Vancouver and drew in more than 3,000 spectators, entrants from Fiji and Japan, as well as US president Jimmy Carter's brother, Billy, as a judge. Annual coverage from NBC TV reached twenty million people.

The World Belly Flop and Cannonball Diving Championship at the Coach House Inn in North Vancouver, 1979.

John Denniston photo

BELOW When Tom Butler talked the prime minister's wife, Margaret Trudeau, into turning up at the opening night of the Daddy Long Legs Disco at the International Plaza Hotel in North Vancouver, her appearance scored national attention for the nightclub. (The former disco is now a Staples office supply store.)

Vancouver Sun, *Bill Keay photo, July 31, 1979*

For a chance to win the coveted Green Bathrobe, a trophy and $1,000 in cash, you had to weigh at least 250 pounds (114 kilograms) to enter. Contestants had to spring off a three-foot (one-metre) diving board and execute two cannonballs and three spread-eagle belly flops. Judges picked a winner based on height of splash, estimated weight of displaced water, artistry and personality.

Trevor Rowe sent me a note when he saw the photo on my blog of his dad Kamikaze Bill leaping from a hot air balloon into the Coach House pool when Trevor was just four years old. His dad, a logger from Bellingham, won second place in the 1979 competition. Trevor says he remembers his dad stuffing weights inside his shirt so that he would meet the minimum weight required to enter. The Miss 1979 Belly Flop was won by Christy Russell, a twenty-six-year-old, 450-pound (200-kilogram) stripper who went by the stage name Big Fannie Annie.

"It's something that is universally understood," Butler told the *Globe and Mail*. "I mean, there's no subtlety to it. But what else can a 300-pound truck driver do and get to have NBC declare that he's champion of the U.S.A.?"

ABOVE Tom Butler with his constant companion, Stuffy, ca. 1988.

Courtesy Andrea Butler

TWINNING THE LIONS GATE BRIDGE

Daien Ide, reference historian at the North Vancouver Museum and Archives, was sitting at her desk one day when she got a tip. A model of a proposed twinned Lions Gate Bridge had turned up at the Burnaby Hospice Thrift Society Store on Kingsway with a $200 price tag. A local had saved the model after finding it tossed out in an alley behind his house a couple of decades earlier. For whatever reason, he decided it needed rehoming and gave it to the thrift shop. The scaled model is clearly identified with the name of the architectural firm—Safdie Architects. Moshe Safdie is a highly regarded architect, known for the Habitat 67 in Montreal, the National Gallery in Ottawa, the Montreal Museum of Fine Arts and our very own Vancouver Public Library Central Branch.

The Lions Gate Bridge spans the first narrows in Burrard Inlet, connects Vancouver to the North Shore and is one of the most iconic structures in the city. Built by the Guinness family to encourage development in West Vancouver, the suspension bridge was tolled from the time it opened in 1938 until 1963. It cost twenty-five cents for cars and five cents for pedestrians. By the early 1990s, the bridge was in serious need of an upgrade or replacement, and three options were proposed. One was to build a tunnel, another was to make the existing three-lane bridge a double-decker and the third was to twin the bridge and double the number of lanes.

Safdie partnered with SNC-Lavalin and the Squamish Nation, which owns the land on the north end of the bridge. The group proposed building an identical bridge to the east of the original structure that would carry northbound traffic, while the original bridge would carry vehicles south into Stanley Park. The new bridge would be tolled, and, judging by the model, would cut a chunk out of Stanley Park. As we now know, the cheapest and least controversial option was chosen, and the existing three-lane bridge was widened and the main bridge deck replaced. In 2005, the Lions Gate Bridge was designated a National Historic Site of Canada. Our traffic problems persist.

Model of the proposed twinned Lions Gate Bridge.
NVMA 2020

THE OTHER TREE IN PRINCESS PARK

Cheryl Hamilton working on *Mirare* at her Granville Island studio.

Michael Vandermeer photo

One of the many things I love about Princess Park in North Vancouver is that there is a tree sculpture hidden in the forest by the stream. I know what you're thinking—doesn't the park already have enough trees? But the sculpture, named *Mirare*, is special. As the plaque says, it is a "sentinel at the forest's edge, inviting us to venture into nature with respect and reverence."

It was not designed for Princess Park, though. The seventeen-foot (5.1-metre) stainless-steel sculpture was cast from a fallen century-old hemlock tree, and it was originally intended for Deep Cove Park. Artists Cheryl Hamilton and Michael Vandermeer won a public art competition with their design after spending a long time studying the area, and made the sculpture in their Granville Island studio. Cheryl has a background in animation, welding and glass blowing. Michael trained as a nuclear physicist but found sculpture more exciting. "It's a lot of the same skills," he says. "You've got to know chemistry and physics and all that stuff to make it work."

Then things got crazy. In the two decades that Cheryl and Michael have worked together they've never experienced anything like it—anger, hate mail, vitriolic messages left on their answering machine. A resident called their prototype a "bong" and said it would corrupt their children. When the artists drove up to the site in their truck, people would stand at their doors and yell at them. A public meeting convened to discuss how the project was a disaster.

"We presented our concept and talked about the process. People stood up and said, 'You are disgusting,' and there was so much anger," says Cheryl. "It's a tree! We were casting a tree." At that point it was obvious that the sculpture wasn't going to work anywhere in Deep Cove.

The budget for *Mirare*, which translates loosely to "look at, to wonder at," was $76,000. The sculpture weighs thousands of pounds, is made from the highest-grade materials and took nearly eight months to create. Cheryl spent three months inside the tube, grinding and polishing to bring up its shiny finish. Michael pulled apart a milling machine to make a special jig so they could drill the holes into the top, and Cheryl welded the pieces together to make it look like bark. "We knew that piece of real estate was so important—important to us and important to the community—and we wanted to make sure that whatever we made was worthy of the location," Cheryl says. "Ironically, it's in a better location."

Mirare in Princess Park.
Michael Vandermeer photo

THE WIGWAM INN AT INDIAN ARM

A few years ago, when I found out that the Deep Cove Heritage Society offered a boat ride up Indian Arm as one of its summer fundraisers, I immediately booked a ticket. I've wanted to see the Wigwam Inn since I started researching its first owner, Alvo von Alvensleben, for my book *At Home with History*. Aside from having a name you couldn't make up, he was the son of a German count, and after having a row with his father, landed in Vancouver in 1904 with just a few dollars in his pocket. He fished for salmon and did other labouring jobs, started speculating in land, and within a few years became a successful financier and developer.

In the early 1900s, Benny Dickens, an advertising manager for the *Daily Province* saw potential in creating a resort at Indian Arm and bought up a few hundred acres of land. He quickly ran out of money and turned to Alvensleben for help. Alvensleben financed the building, changed the theme from Indigenous to German and created a *Luftkurort* (fresh-air resort). It attracted guests such as American millionaires John D. Rockefeller and John Jacob Astor, before he went down with the *Titanic* in 1912.

Unless you own a boat, Indian Arm is fairly inaccessible, yet that wasn't always the case. In 1910, the year the Wigwam Inn opened, there were four different sternwheelers taking guests up and down the arm from Vancouver. Alvensleben was selling lots for $200 to $300 and promising a private boat service to Vancouver that guaranteed to get business people to the office by nine a.m.

When the First World War hit, Alvensleben became an enemy alien and the government seized all of his property. The Inn

Wigwam Inn, ca. 1912.
Vancouver Archives
LGN 1028

was sold and changed hands many times, and it all but disappeared from public view until the early 1960s when William "Fats" Robertson and his lawyer Rockmill "Rocky" Myers took control.

Robertson had paid $60,000 for the Wigwam Inn and his plan was to turn it into a swanky casino and brothel for the rich, who could afford to lose $30,000 or $40,000 a night in a private game.

On Saturday, July 28, 1962, Marine Constable Gale Gardner and others from the Gibsons RCMP detachment were ordered to report to HMCS *Discovery* at Deadman's Island in Coal Harbour. When they arrived, they met up with a second

police boat full of officers from the liquor, gambling and prostitution squads, as well as general investigators, senior members of the force and a police dog. They arranged to leave Deadman's Island so they would arrive at the Wigwam Inn just after midnight. "Timing was essential so that the raid could take place early Sunday morning, because then all activities at the inn would be illegal," Gale told me. "When we were close, all the running lights were shut down and our vessels were moored at the marine dock. Then members rushed ashore and all hell broke loose."

Robertson, age thirty-four, was arrested and put in the galley of one of the RCMP boats. Twenty-three-year-old Gale was

Wigwam Inn, 2017.
Eve Lazarus photo

sent to guard him. "Even today, I can still see the forlorn Fats Robertson sitting there, his empire busted," says the former RCMP officer.

RCMP found a large quantity of gambling paraphernalia, stolen paintings and antiques, plates for printing counterfeit money and 300 cases of beer.

Fats Robertson and thirty-year-old Rocky Myers were charged with conspiring to bribe Corporal Jack McDonald of the RCMP drug squad. They were sentenced to six years in jail. After his release, Robertson lost his trading privileges on the Vancouver Stock Exchange for manipulating the share price of two junior mining companies. He was back in the headlines again when he was caught heading up a major drug trafficking ring. Police seized over $4 million worth of cocaine, and Robertson was convicted and sentenced to prison, this time for twenty-three years. He was out in eight, had his trading privileges reinstated and in 2003 was back in the news yet again when a former insurance salesman from West Vancouver who moonlighted as a hit man said Robertson had contracted his services for two murders in 1969.

As for the Wigwam Inn, the Royal Vancouver Yacht Club bought the inn in 1985. Now it's strictly for members only.

BUNTZEN POWER PROJECT

When I took a boat ride up Indian Arm in 2017 to see the Wigwam Inn, I didn't realize that another highlight of the trip would be seeing the two massive power stations that dominate the eastern shore of Buntzen Bay.

Heather Virtue-Lapierre was born there in 1943. Her grandfather Matt Virtue was one of the first powerhouse operators shortly after station number one opened in 1903. Her father, Jim, carried on the family tradition from 1941 until the plant was automated in 1953. Heather's school was a one-room building above the powerhouse. She says that powerhouse operators were exempt from service during the war years and instead joined the Pacific Coast Militia Rangers. "Nobody was allowed to land at Buntzen without permission during the war," she says. "I still remember the blackout curtains in our house."

When Heather stayed with her grandparents in Vancouver, her parents put her on the MV *Scenic* under the care of Captain James Anderson. The boat was a floating post office that brought mail to the isolated population along Burrard Inlet and Indian Arm and ferried passengers back and forth. Captain Anderson would make sure Heather was delivered to her grandparents at the foot of Gore Avenue.

Dawson Truax's father also worked at the power station. Dawson was just eighteen months old when he moved to Buntzen with his war-bride mother in 1946. "My mother talked about it quite a bit. It was quite horrifying for her to move from London, England, to the Canadian wilderness," he says. The family lived in a cabin on the hill above the power plant owned by the BC Electric Railway (the forerunner to BC Hydro). "It was quite a small community and only took three men to run the power plant at any time over three shifts a day," Dawson says. "There was a hoist on tracks that went up the hill from the plant area to the cabin. One of my first childhood memories is of my father putting me on the hoist with a pile of parcels while he walked alongside."

Buntzen gets its name from Johannes Buntzen, the first general manager of the BCER. But the power stations weren't the first industry on the arm. There was a Japanese logging camp in the area as early as 1880. Between 1902 and 1914, around 500 men camped there while they worked on a tunnel from Coquitlam Lake to Buntzen Lake.

Vancouver's rapid growth soon demanded more power, and power station number two opened in 1914. Rumour has it, the infamous architect Francis Rattenbury designed number two, and it does look like his work. But it's not true. The second powerhouse was designed by Robert Lyon, an architect employed by the BCER.

TOP Far left: Matt Virtue; H.R. Heinrich, master mechanic, is in the cap; #5 Tom Lundy; #6 George Henshaw; #8 Jim Findlay, 1910.
Courtesy Heather Virtue-Lapierre

BOTTOM The second generation—from left: Jim Virtue (son of Matt), Vic Shorting, George Mantle, Gill McLaughlin, Bill Henshaw (son of George), ca. 1940.
Courtesy Heather Virtue-Lapierre

1 Buntzen Powerhouse #1, 1913.
Courtesy Heather Virtue-Lapierre

2 Power Station #1.
Eve Lazarus photo, July 2017

3 Power Station #2.
Eve Lazarus photo, July 2017

4 Buntzen Powerhouse #2, 1913.
Courtesy Heather Virtue-Lapierre

THE DOLLARTON PLEASURE FAIRE AND MAPLEWOOD MUD FLATS

I was first introduced to the work of photographer Bruce Stewart and the history of the Maplewood Flats in 2015 when I was doing some research at the North Vancouver Museum and Archives. The Archives had an exhibit called *West of Eden* and it showed Stewart's remarkable black and white photography taken over a two-week period in 1972. Instead of the usual wood ducks, chickadees and the odd deer I'm used to seeing in the conservation area, there were small children running free, hippies soaking up the sun and portraits of young and old, naked and clothed, in front of the incongruous backdrop of the Chevron oil refinery.

In that era of rapid urban redevelopment and civic unrest, the Dollarton Pleasure Faire was one of many "faires" that popped up around North American in the late 1960s and '70s. It was meant to be a celebration of alternative living timed to clash

The mud flats in 1971.
Tony Westman photo,
NVMA 15825

Dollarton Pleasure Faire.
Bruce Stewart photo, 1972,
NVMA 042

with the corporate culture of the Pacific National Exhibition that was held across the inlet.

The two-week counterculture faire was also a show of support—the mud-flat squatter community versus the District of North Vancouver, which just the year before had razed a number of homes near the tideline, evicted the occupants and promised to soon replace everything with a hotel and a shopping mall.

The land, which is almost a third the size of Stanley Park and situated just east of the Ironworkers Memorial Bridge, has a long history. The mud flats provided a fishing ground for the Tsleil-Waututh Nation, and from the 1920s, a sand and gravel company operated a quarry here. In the 1960s, the floors and buildings from demolished West End heritage houses were barged over, mixed with logs and garbage from the inlet, and used as fill on the mud flats. Later that decade, a community of squatters—many of them artists and environmentalists—moved in and built shacks from salvaged materials above the tidal mud flats. The majority of the shacks had no electricity or running water.

Maplewood Flats during the Dollarton Pleasure Faire, 1972.
Bruce Stewart photo, NVMA 034

The squatter village partially survived until 1973, when, with the exception of one shack belonging to Mike Bozzer, the unofficial mayor of Maplewood, the remaining structures were destroyed. Bozzer managed to hang on to his home until 1981, when the district decided it didn't meet public health standards and destroyed it as well. Public outrage quashed the development of the flats and today the area is a wildlife refuge. The only evidence of its past is artist Ken Lum's miniature replicas of three of the mud flats' cabins, placed there after the 2010 Winter Olympics.

GRAIN ELEVATORS, A FIRE AND A GHOST STORY

A little before ten a.m. on October 3, 1975, David Samson, an inspector with the Canadian Grain Commission, was walking down the train tracks to the Burrard terminals when he saw a few of the workers he knew moving quickly away from the grain elevators.

"The side of the workhouse terminal had been blown off, and I could see the stairs going all the way up to the top of the grain elevator," he says. "There wasn't any real blaze at that time, but that came in the next half hour." A conveyor belt had caught fire and ignited the explosive grain dust in the elevator. Grain dust, David tells me, is about thirty-five times more explosive than TNT.

Ed Hooper was standing at the top of the elevator when the fire broke out, and he grabbed a fire extinguisher and tried to put it out. David thinks the second explosion must have killed Hooper because nothing of him was ever found.

The two explosions rocked North Vancouver. Sherri Hunt-Todd clearly remembers hearing them all the way at her house in West Vancouver's British Properties. David Ferman was on a grade four field trip to the Old Spaghetti Factory restaurant in Gastown. "I remember seeing a bright yellow light through the north window," he says. "I thought something had blown up in Burrard Inlet, or that a lightning bolt had hit a ship. Then came the sound—a muffled boom—and the yellow light became an orange fireball that blew outward towards us before quickly receding under grey clouds."

Heather Virtue-Lapierre was watching the fire from the bluff at the bottom of St. Davids Avenue on the North Shore. "The heat was so intense that there was burning

The fire killed five men, severely burned twelve others, caused $8 million in damages and destroyed the workhouse, track shed and a large part of the shipping gallery in the former Moodyville area.

NVMA 16021

barley flying around and it left marks on our truck that was parked behind the substation up on Fourth Street," she says. "The firemen eventually moved us back because they were afraid there might be another explosion. People were hosing down their roofs to keep them from catching fire."

"The workhouse was made of wood, so eventually the whole thing caught fire," says David. "Mel Hoey was standing on the grate when the explosion took place. He had these big heavy workboots on, and all the other clothes that he was wearing were burned right off."

Other men came staggering out of the elevator covered in dirt and burns. Sixteen men suffered severe burns, and four later died in hospital. They were Hoey, fifty-eight; John Scully, fifty-six; James Evoy, forty-two; and twenty-eight-year-old Dave Brown.

When registered nurse Liisa Rowat started her eleven p.m. shift on the fourth floor of the Fairview Pavilion at Vancouver General Hospital on the night of the explosion, she found the eighteen-bed burn unit in organized chaos. The corridors were full of stretchers, and extra staff had been called in so every burn patient could have his own nurse. One patient, she remembers, had burns covering ninety percent of his body.

Dave Brown was taken to the burn unit at VGH, where, against all odds, he managed to survive for fifty-eight days, before dying of his injuries. Then, for some reason, it seems the young man decided to stick around in his room—415.

In 1989, Robert Belyk researched the story as part of his book *Ghosts: True Tales of Eerie Encounters*. Although eleven years had passed, Belyk was able to find two nurses and a patient who said they had experienced strange encounters with Brown's ghost.

Staff told Belyk that they heard breathing when no one was in the room. They would feel a presence, see an unexplained shape in the room. The toilet would flush, the lights would go on and off and the room was often freezing cold. Staff said that although it was unsettling, they never felt any danger. The ghost was kind to other burn patients. He would visit critically ill patients and bring them comfort, they said. The ghost apparently stayed around the burn unit until 1983, when staff moved to new facilities, and the building was torn down two years later.

ACKNOWLEDGMENTS

A huge thank-you to Michael Kluckner for not only helping kick around the structure and look for this book at the idea stage, but for taking on the unedited manuscript, correcting my mistakes and providing encouragement, coffee and cookies. Angus McIntyre, thank you for sharing your memories of Vancouver and allowing me to publish so many of your fabulous photos.

As always, thanks to the Belshaw gang, especially Tom Carter for listening and for your generosity supplying photos, ephemera, advice and fact-checking; and to Cat Rose, Jason Vanderhill, Will Woods, Lani Russwurm and Aaron Chapman for help along the way. Neil Whaley, thank you for allowing me to run several pieces from your collection.

I'd also like to thank the following for help with various aspects of the book: Jacqueline Allan, Bill Allman, John Atkin, David Banks, Kate Bird, Andrea Butler, Bob Cain, Andy Cassidy, Chuck Currie, Marcus Dell, John Denniston, Paul Dixon, Rob Frith, Judy Graves, Maurice Guibord, Cheryle Harrison, Glen Hodges, Maria and Rick Iaci, Don Luxton, Murray Maisey, Nathan Mawby, Gregory Melle, Andrea Nicholson, Lisa Pantages, Pamela Post, Lisa Smith, Chris Stiles, Mark Truelove, Jim Wolf and David Wong.

It would be impossible to write a book on local history without the help and resources of the various archives, museums and public libraries. I was able to include so many historical photos because of the generosity of Vancouver Archives and its massive digital collection of photographs. Thanks to Karen Dearlove and Jessica Bushey at North Vancouver Museum and Archives; Jessica Quan at the Vancouver Heritage Foundation; Patrick Gunn at Heritage Vancouver; the Vancouver Police Museum and Archives; and the Vancouver Historical Society. Thanks also go to Teresa Sudeyko and Jana Tyner at the Morris and Helen Belkin Art Gallery; Christina Hedlund, Simon Fraser University Galleries; and Erwin Wodarczak, UBC archivist. Sourcing photos during the time of COVID-19 was particularly challenging because so many libraries and archives were in lockdown. My utmost appreciation goes to research librarians Carolyn Soltau at the *Vancouver Sun* and *Province* and the NVMA's Daien Ide. You are truly archival rock stars!

My deep gratitude goes to the British Columbia Arts Council and to Vancouver Heritage Foundation and the Yosef Wosk Publication Grant that went toward the writing and photos for *Vancouver Exposed*.

I'm especially grateful to my amazing team at Arsenal Pulp Press. Thank you, Brian Lam, Robert Ballantyne, marketing mavens Cynara Geissler (Arsenal) and Ariel Hudnall (ZG Communications), my editor Shirarose Wilensky and newest staffer Jazmin Welch, who has made my book so beautiful.

NOTES

DOWNTOWN

1 George Peloquin. "Voters Say 'Go' for Super-block." *Vancouver Sun*, May 23, 1968, 1.

2 "Vancouver's First Station Still Stands." *Vancouver Sun*, November 5, 1948, 10.

3 Jill Wade. "'A Palace for the Public': Housing Reform and the 1946 Occupation of the Old Hotel Vancouver." *BC Studies* no. 69/70 (Spring/Summer 1986): 305–9.

4 Aileen Campbell. "His Monuments Remain— But Who Was Marega?" *Province*, February 28, 1975, 37.

5 "Artists Were Pioneers." *Province*, August 1, 1975, 32.

6 *Ibid.*

7 "Bank Building Gets Bronze Sculpture." *Vancouver Sun*, April 22, 1968, 2.

8 Vancouver has had three Orpheum Theatres that ran Orpheum Circuit Vaudeville. The first was the Orpheum owned by Sullivan and Considine on 805 West Pender Street (originally the Alhambra, then the Royal, then the People's Theatre, then the Orpheum in 1906). The second was the Orpheum (the Vancouver Opera House renamed by Sullivan and Considine), and the third is our current Orpheum Theatre on Granville Street, which was built in 1927.

9 "Considine Brothers, Seattle Gamblers, Must Answer for Death of Ex-Chief of Police Meredith." *Morning Union* (Grass Valley, California), June 28, 1901, 1.

10 Aileen Campbell. "The Golden Age of the Wrecker." *Province,* May 17, 1969, 5.

11 "Movie Projectionist Escapes Death When Bomb Wrecks Auto." *Vancouver Sun*, January 22, 1932, 1.

12 Noel Robinson. "Miss Mollison of Glencoe Lodge." *Province*, May 25, 1946, 31.

13 Aileen Campbell. "His Monuments Remain— But Who Was Marega?" *Province*, February 28, 1975, 37.

14 "Art, Works Not Same, Experts Remind Chant." *Province*, March 3, 1966, 5.

15 Les Wedman. "The Lady Who Won't Go Away." *Vancouver Sun*, September 5, 1969, 80.

16 *Vancouver Sun*, March 17, 1945, 5.

17 Jack Shadbolt. "Post Office—Failure." *Vancouver Sun*, March 21, 1958, 4.

18 Warnett Kennedy. *Vancouver Tomorrow: A Search for Greatness*. Vancouver: Mitchell Press, 1974.

DOWNTOWN EASTSIDE

1 "Department of Public Works Rule of the Road." *Province*, July 14, 1920, 17.

2 *Vancouver Sun*, May 15, 1952, 30.

3 George Classen. "It's Still Our Tallest." *Vancouver Sun*, June 11, 1955, 59.

4 *Canadian Rail: The Magazine of Canada's Railway History* no. 534 (January–February 2010): 3.

5 R. Monro St. John. "B.C's First Aviator." *Province*, December 12, 1956, 56.

6 Aubrey F. Roberts. "Vancouver's First Aviator Recalls His Initial Flight." *Province*, April 27, 1930, 43.

7 C.W. Gilchrist. "Roads and Highways." *Canadian Encyclopedia*, last updated March 4, 2015. https://www.thecanadianencyclopedia.ca/en/article/roads-and-highways

8 F.W. Luce. "Level Tracks an Asset." *Vancouver Daily World*, May 11, 1923, 11.

9 *Vancouver Sun*, editorial, January 16, 1929, 8.

10 Hadani Ditmars. "Top 10 Hotels in Vancouver." *The Guardian*, July 29, 2015, https://www.theguardian.com/travel/2015/jul/29/top-10-hotels-vancouver-canada

WEST END

1 "English Bay Drive to Become Reality." *Vancouver Sun*, June 13, 1950, 16.

2 "Let's Save Englesea Lodge!" *Vancouver Sun*, January 16, 1980, 5.

3 Steve Berry. "Two Explosions Heard before Fire." *Province*, February 2, 1981, 3.

4 Steve Berry. "Curious Parallel Eyed by Alderman Kennedy." *Province*, February 2, 1981, 1.

5 Aileen Campbell. "On the Beach." *Province*, August 4, 1973, 49.

6 *Ibid.*

7 Moira Farrow. "Innovators, Battle Wreckers." *Vancouver Sun*, May 24, 1973, 20.

8 "Colour Bar Removed from Crystal Pool." *Province*, November 6, 1945, 8.

9 Chester Grant. "Harry's Campaigning to Save Crystal Pool." *Vancouver Sun*, December 3, 1966, 23.

10 "Maxine Beauty Students Are from All Quarters of the Globe." *Edmonton Journal*, July 8, 1937, 7.

11 Aaron Chapman. *Vancouver After Dark: The Wild History of a City's Nightlife.* Vancouver: Arsenal Pulp Press, 2019, 110.

12 Karenn Krangle. "Council Gives Stuart Building Last Rites." *Vancouver Sun*, June 30, 1982, 9.

13 Barb Wood in an email to Jason Vanderhill in 2012.

14 City of Vancouver ParkFinder. "Devonian Harbour Park." https://covapp.vancouver.ca/parkfinder/parkdetail.aspx?inparkid=18

15 Patti Flather. "Man of Stone." *Vancouver Sun*, March 29, 1986, 17.

16 "Matthews Goes to Bat to Save Tim's Place." *Vancouver Sun*, March 13, 1958, 29.

17 "The Lesson at Tim's Place." *Vancouver Sun*, May 6, 1959, 4.

18 "Tim's Place A-Rotting." *Vancouver Sun*, November 19, 1963, 25.

WEST OF MAIN STREET

1   Robert Williamson. "Gardener Tends Oasis in Concrete Wilderness." *Globe and Mail*, May 13, 1993, 17.

2   John Mackie. "Lost in Transition." *Vancouver Sun*, June 23, 2007, 33.

3   "Youth Insane in Axe Murders." *Province*, February 17, 1967, 10.

4   Jake Van der Kamp. "Boy Who Killed Family Now a 'Model Citizen No Danger to Society.'" *Vancouver Sun*, September 17, 1977, 45.

5   Clancy Loranger. *Province* [column], December 2, 1982, 22.

6   Chuck Davis. "Reclusive Champion Was Feted by Crowds but Later Took His Own Life." *Province*, November 29, 2004, 29.

7   Bob McConnell. "3 Die as Ship Rips BC Ferry." *Province*, August 3, 1970, 1, and "3 Die on BC Ship BC Ferry." *Vancouver Sun*, August 3, 1970, 1.

EAST OF MAIN STREET

1   Eve Lazarus. *Blood, Sweat, and Fear: The Story of Inspector Vance, Vancouver's First Forensic Investigator.* Vancouver: Arsenal Pulp Press, 2017, 57.

2   "Hastings Park 1942." http://hastingspark1942.ca/buildings-overview/livestock-building/

3   Jean Howarth. "Makes Prison Look Like Luxury Hotel." *Province*, October 29, 1954, 29.

4   Simma Holt. "Press Invited to Probe Girls School." *Vancouver Sun*, April 27, 1956, 1.

NORTH VANCOUVER

1   Glenn Bohn. "Innovative Architect Receives Award for Heritage Conservation." *Vancouver Sun*, February 26, 1998, B2.

2   "Squamish Mission, North Vancouver, Is Point of Interest." *Province*, August 14, 1909, 25.

3   *Ibid.*

4   "St. Paul's (BC)." Indian Residential School History & Dialogue Centre, University of British Columbia. https://collections.irshdc.ubc.ca/index.php/Detail/entities/56

5   William Nahanee, oral history, North Vancouver Museum and Archives, 2015. *Voices and Views*, 201–65.

6   "Intruder Seen in Convent Where Woman Strangled." *Vancouver Sun*, December 18, 1973, 1.

7   Elizabeth Withey. "Closing Doors." *Alberta Views*, October 1, 2007.

8   Ian Haysom. "Vancouver PR Man Was Master of Photo Op." *Globe and Mail*, July 26, 2013, S10.

BIBLIOGRAPHY

BOOKS

Atkin, John, and Andy Coupland. *The Changing City: Architecture and History Walking Tours in Central Vancouver*. Vancouver: Stellar Press, 2010.

Belyk, Robert C. *Ghosts: True Tales of Eerie Encounters*. Vancouver: TouchWood Editions, 1990.

Boles, Glen W., William Lowell Putnam, and Roger W. Laurilla. *Canadian Mountain Place Names: The Rockies and Columbia Mountains*. Calgary: Rocky Mountain Books, 2006.

Chapman, Aaron. *Liquor, Lust and the Law: The Story of Vancouver's Legendary Penthouse Nightclub*. Vancouver: Arsenal Pulp Press, 2012.

_____. *Vancouver After Dark: The Wild History of a City's Nightlife*. Vancouver: Arsenal Pulp Press, 2019.

Cruise, David, and Alison Griffiths. *Fleecing the Lamb: The Inside Story of the Vancouver Stock Exchange*. Vancouver: Douglas & McIntyre, 1987.

Davies, David Llewelyn, and Lorne H. Nicklason. *The CPR's English Bay Branch: The Intended Terminus of the Canadian Pacific Railway*. BC Rail Guide No. 8. Canadian Railroad Historical Association, 1975.

Davis, Chuck (ed.). *The Chuck Davis History of Metropolitan Vancouver*. Madeira Park, BC: Harbour Publishing, 2011.

_____. *The Greater Vancouver Book*. Vancouver: The Linkman Press, 1997.

Farley, Lilias, Irene Hoffar Reid, Beatrice Lennie, and Vera Weatherbie (eds.). *First Class: Four Graduates from the Vancouver School of Decorative and Applied Arts, 1929*. Vancouver: Floating Curatorial Gallery/Women in Focus, 1987.

Fralic, Shelley. *Making Headlines: 100 Years of the Vancouver Sun*. Kelowna: Sandhill Book Marketing, 2012.

Francis, Daniel. *L.D.: Mayor Louis Taylor and the Rise of Vancouver*. Vancouver: Arsenal Pulp Press, 2004.

Gutstein, Donald. *Vancouver Ltd.* Toronto: James Lorimer & Company, 1975.

Hawley, Samuel. *I Just Ran: Percy Williams, World's Fastest Human*. Vancouver: Ronsdale Press, 2011.

Holmlund, Mona. *Inspiring Women: A Celebration of Herstory*. Regina: Coteau Books, 2003.

Kalman, Harold, and Robin Ward. *Exploring Vancouver: The Architectural Guide*. Vancouver: Douglas & McIntyre, 2012.

Kennedy, Warnett. *Vancouver Tomorrow: A Search for Greatness*. Vancouver: Mitchell Press, 1974.

Kluckner, Michael. *Vancouver Remembered*. Vancouver: Whitecap Books, 2011.

_____. *Vanishing Vancouver: The Last 25 Years*. Vancouver: Whitecap Books, 2012.

Kopytek, Bruce Allen. *Eaton's: The Trans-Canada Store*. Cheltenham, UK: The History Press, 2014.

Lazarus, Eve. *At Home with History: The Untold Secrets of Greater Vancouver's Heritage Homes*. Vancouver: Anvil Press, 2007.

_____. *Blood, Sweat, and Fear: The Story of Inspector Vance, Vancouver's First Forensic Investigator*. Vancouver: Arsenal Pulp Press, 2017.

_____. *Cold Case Vancouver: The City's Most Baffling Unsolved Murders*. Vancouver: Arsenal Pulp Press, 2015.

_____. *Frommer's with Kids Vancouver*. Toronto: CDG Books Canada, 2000.

_____. *Murder by Milkshake: An Astonishing True Story of Adultery, Arsenic, and a Charismatic Killer*. Vancouver: Arsenal Pulp Press, 2018.

_____. *Sensational Vancouver*. Vancouver: Anvil Press, 2014.

_____. *Sensational Victoria: Bright Lights, Red Lights, Murders, Ghosts & Gardens*. Vancouver: Anvil Press, 2012.

Liscombe, Rhodri Winson. *The New Spirit: Modern Architecture in Vancouver, 1938–1963*. Cambridge: MIT Press, 1997.

Luxton, Donald (ed.). *Building the West: The Early Architects of British Columbia*. Vancouver: Talonbooks, 2003.

McQueen, Rod. *The Eatons: The Rise and Fall of Canada's Royal Family*. Toronto: Stoddart Publishing, 1998.

Reksten, Terry. *Rattenbury*. Victoria: Sono Nis Press, 1978.

Scullion, Bob, and Fred Thirkell. *Philip Timms' Vancouver: 1900–1910*. Victoria: Heritage House Publishing, 2006.

Smith, Lisa Anne, and Barbara Rogers. *Our Friend Joe: The Joe Fortes Story*. Vancouver: Ronsdale Press, 2012.

Steil, John, and Aileen Stalker. *Public Art in Vancouver: Angels among Lions*. Victoria: Touchwood Editions, 2009.

Walker, Elizabeth. *Street Names of Vancouver*. Vancouver: Vancouver Historical Society, 1999.

MEDIA

Amarillo Globe-Times

Calgary Herald

CBC

Daily Province

Edmonton Journal

Evening Review (Ohio)

Georgia Straight

Globe and Mail

The Guardian

Harrisburg Telegraph

Herald News

Interior News

Morning Union (Grass Valley, California)

National Post

Nebraska State Journal

North Shore News

Spokane Chronicle

Star Phoenix

Surrey Leader

Times Colonist

Tyee

Vancouver Courier

Vancouver Daily World

Vancouver News Herald

Vancouver Sun

Victoria Daily Times

ARTICLES

Barrett, Tom. "Labor and the Arts." *Vancouver Sun*, April 25, 1991, 82.

"Binning Mural Finds New Home at UBC." *UBC Reports*, April 20, 1989, 2.

Chong, Jeffrey. "If Logs Could Talk: A Brief History of Stanley Park." *AuthentiCity* (City of Vancouver Archives blog), July 7, 2011. https://www.vancouverarchives.ca/2011/07/07/if-logs-could-talk-a-brief-introduction-to-stanley-park/

Ewert, Henry. "BC Electric Rail Company Ltd." *Canadian Rail: The Magazine of Canada's Railway History* 534, January–February 2010, 3.

Glegg, Alastair. "A Life in Education: Margaret Bayne and the Vancouver Girls' Industrial School." *Historical Studies in Education*, Fall 2006, 201–24. https://historicalstudiesineducation.ca/index.php/edu_hse-rhe/article/view/350/427

Guibord, Maurice Conrad. "The Evolution of Chinese Graves at Burnaby's Ocean View Cemetery: From Stigmatized Purlieu to Political Adaptations and Cultural Identity." M.A. thesis, Simon Fraser University Department of History, Faculty of Arts and Social Sciences, 2013.

Hall, Neal. "Life of an Alleged Contract Killer." *Ottawa Citizen*, July 21, 2003, A3.

Hawthorn, Tom. "Killer Corbett: The Day the Local Police Cornered the FBI's Most Wanted." *Province*, October 29, 1990, 10.

MacDonald, Norbert. "The Canadian Pacific Railway and Vancouver's Development to 1900." *BC Studies*, 35, Autumn 1977, 3–35.

Monteyne, David. "From Canvas to Concrete in Fifty Years." *BC Studies*, 124, Winter 1999–2000, 41–68.

Rumen, Nina. "Vancouver's Monuments to Nurses." *RNABC History of Nursing Group*, 2016. https://bcnursinghistory.ca/wp-content/uploads/2016/08/monumentspresentation.pdf

"A Short History of Interurbans in the Lower Mainland." *The Buzzer*, March 24, 2009. https://buzzer.translink.ca/2009/03/a-short-history-of-interurbans-in-the-lower-mainland/

Todd, Robert B. "The Organization of Professional Theatre in Vancouver, 1886–1914." *BC Studies* 44, Winter 1979–80, 3–20.

Wade, Jill. "'A Palace for the Public': Housing Reform and the 1946 Occupation of the Old Hotel Vancouver." *BC Studies* 69/70, Spring/Summer 1986, 305–9.

Withey, Elizabeth. "Closing Doors." *Alberta Views*, October 1, 2007.

REPORTS

City of Vancouver, *Redevelopment in Downtown Vancouver*, Report #5, July 21, 1964.

Frontier to Freeway: A Short Illustrated History of the Roads in British Columbia. Ministry of Transportation and Highways. https://www2.gov.bc.ca/assets/gov/driving-and-transportation/reports-and-reference/reports-and-studies/frontier_to_freeway.pdf

Harland Bartholomew and Associates, *A Plan for the City of Vancouver, British Columbia*, 1928.

Various reports by the National Centre for Truth and Reconciliation, University of Manitoba, 2015.

Third Annual Report, Provincial Industrial School for Girls, Superintendent, Victoria, BC, 1917.

Twenty-second Annual Report of the Provincial Industrial Home for Girls of the Province of British Columbia, April 1, 1935, to March 31, 1936.

WEBSITES

Hastings Park 1942: http://hastingspark1942.ca/buildings-overview/livestock-building/

Heritage Vancouver: http://heritagevancouver.org/

Illustrated Vancouver: https://illustratedvancouver.ca/

Past Tense: https://pasttensevancouver.wordpress.com/

Price Tags: https://pricetags.ca/

Streetcars before Buses: British Columbia Electric Railway, UBC Digitization Project: https://digitize.library.ubc.ca/digitizers-blog/streetcars-before-buses-british-columbia-electric-railway/

Vancouver as It Was: A Photo History Journey: https://vanasitwas.wordpress.com/

West End Vancouver: https://westendvancouver.wordpress.com/streets-i-to-z/nelson-street/2000-block-nelson-street/2050-nelson-street/

INDEX

Photo by
Rebecca Blissett

Eve Lazarus is a North Vancouver–based journalist and author. Her passion for true crime and non-traditional history has led to nine books of non-fiction, including Arsenal titles and BC bestsellers *Murder by Milkshake* (2018); *Blood, Sweat, and Fear* (2017); and *Cold Case Vancouver* (2015). Her books have garnered six nominations including finalist for Best National True Crime book (Arthur Ellis Awards), the Bill Duthie Booksellers' Choice Award (BC Book Prizes) and the City of Vancouver Book Award. *Sensational Vancouver* (2014) was the recipient of a City of Vancouver Heritage Award. Eve continues to blog obsessively at *Every Place Has a Story.* *evelazarus.com*

ALSO BY EVE LAZARUS

At Home with History: The Untold Secrets of Greater Vancouver's Heritage Homes (Anvil Press, 2007)

Blood, Sweat, and Fear: The Story of Inspector Vance, Vancouver's First Forensic Investigator (Arsenal Pulp Press, 2017)

Cold Case Vancouver: The City's Most Baffling Unsolved Murders (Arsenal Pulp Press, 2015)

Frommer's with Kids Vancouver (CDG Books Canada, 2000)

The Life and Art of Frank Molnar, Jack Hardman and LeRoy Jensen (Mother Tongue Publishing, 2009)

Murder by Milkshake: An Astonishing True Story of Adultery, Arsenic, and a Charismatic Killer (Arsenal Pulp Press, 2018)

Sensational Vancouver (Anvil Press, 2014)

Sensational Victoria: Bright Lights, Red Lights, Murders, Ghosts & Gardens (Anvil Press, 2012)